Kitchen Witchin'

Thoughts, Tricks, and Recipes

P. B. Owl

a BlackWyrm book
Louisville, Kentucky

KITCHEN WITCHIN': THOUGHTS, TRICKS, AND RECIPES

Copyright ©2015 by BlackWyrm Publishing

All rights reserved, including the right to reproduce this book, or portion thereof, in any form. Written permission must be secured from the publisher to use or reproduce any part of this book, except for brief quotations in critical reviews or articles.

A BlackWyrm Book
BlackWyrm Publishing
10307 Chimney Ridge Ct, Louisville, KY 40299

Printed in the United States of America.

ISBN: 978-1-61318-172-0

Cover and author photos: Wayne "Thag" Walls
Photo design: P. B. Owl
Photoshop for front cover: A. M. Stephens

First edition: April 2015

Dedicated to:

Kirsdarke, who said I should keep writing no matter what

Rhea, Rhiannon, and Starrah, Priestesses, Ladies,
and Kitchen Witches all

BlackWyrm Publications, for believing in me

The WynDragon Tradition of Wicca,
in all its Incarnations and Avatars

MoonTurtle, who had a "round tuit" in her pocket

Eleanor, who would have loved this

Thag Jenkins, because it is all his fault

Disclaimer

This book was written by an old, cranky Kitchen Witch who is opinionated, rude, foul-mouthed, and about as non PC as you can get and still be Pagan. I would probably be thrown out of more gatherings, festivals, and Sabbat celebrations if it wasn't for the fact I cook so d*mn well. Parts of this book will offend carnivores, omnivores, vegetarians, and Vegans (I make fun of all food choices). Much of this book is peppered with jokes that are crude and could be deemed offensive. I want the reader to get a real feel for this calling and my history in it, and that means being genuine enough that the feeling you get through this work almost has its own smells and tastes. I have sanitized some words or statements slightly, and if you don't like the methodology for doing so, you can kiss my *terix. The people mentioned in this book are mostly not fictional, but I am aware this is almost beyond belief. All names used here are Craft names or nicknames, to protect the privacy of the individuals involved. All true stories or quotes are given for illustrative purposes, and in some cases names have been withheld so that people don't have to put bags over their heads in shame.

Table of Contents

Blessing the Food 1
General Etiquette Toward the Kitchen and the Kitchen Witch 2
Tricks 5
    Kitchen Tricks 6
    People Tricks 8
    Health Tricks 9
    Ingredient Tricks 11
    Inventory Tricks 16
    Liquid Tricks 20
How to Use Affordable Foods People Make Fun of to Feed
    Large Groups 22
Ten Things That Ruin Food at Gatherings 27
Kitchen Witch Ten Commandments 31
The Ten Weirdest Things I've Seen as a Kitchen Witch 32
Recipes 35
MTAQ (MoonTurtle Asked Questions) 54
Conclusion 64
Glossary of Terms 65
References and Suggested Reading 70

Introduction

The book you are holding is one part cook book, one part memoir, one part joke book, and one part a very specialized Book of Shadows. It is a story, told from one old Kitchen Witch to a lot of other Kitchen Witches, some I will never meet, some who don't yet know they are called to be Kitchen Witches, and even some who haven't been born yet. It's a story I'm still learning, after first hearing it while looking up at my grandmother's stove. It's an introduction to a calling, and a way of life.

What is a Kitchen Witch?

In general, a Kitchen Witch is anyone whose magical and spiritual contributions to their family, coven, circle, or community are significantly expressed through the preparation of food and the nourishment of bodies (without which incarnate souls become disincarnate souls and much less likely to achieve practical results). If you've not tried to do it yourself, believe me when I say that feeding more than 20 people at a time on a limited budget is a magical act equal to anything you have seen in a more formal ritual setting. How do you identify a Kitchen Witch (or know that you should self identify as one)? A Kitchen Witch may be an herbalist, vintner, or brewer of some skill, but this should not be assumed. Many who self identify as Kitchen Witches are also gatherers, gardeners, farmers, raisers of livestock, or hunters (fishermen are hunters who get wet). Many Kitchen Witches are concerned with sustainability in a variety of forms, so they advocate for reuse, repurposing, and recycling (in that order), and are harsh critics of waste. Some Kitchen Witches promote only organic food choices, including the preparation of only those foods that are growth hormone free and non gene modified. Extreme couponing and bargain hunting are common signs of the Kitchen Witch in action. If your athame is used to chop food and your wooden spoon is consecrated to the Goddess, you might be a Kitchen Witch.

Note: The reason the term Kitchen Witch is capitalized in this book like God, Goddess, Lord, Lady, the Sabbats, or other Wiccan titles, is that it really is as important a concept, and as close to the workings of who and what we are, and can be, as any of these others. A Kitchen Witch is an avatar. A Kitchen Witch creates magic with every choice, working toward the ultimate goal of nourishing. This is a holy calling, and if I am irreverent in my descriptions, and in relating my experiences, this does not make the calling any less holy. (It just proves that in my own self, I'm not very holy, and that my sense of humor is low and vulgar.)

In terms of spiritual belief, a Kitchen Witch is likely to honor Goddesses of grain, like Cornwoman or Ceres, Gods and Goddesses of the Hunt, like Herne and Diana, Gods of wine such as Bacchus, or a Divinity of plenty, like the Dagda. You will likely find representations of food and plenty on the altar of a Kitchen Witch, including sheaves of grain, ears of corn, a cornucopia filled with fruits and vegetables (the horn of plenty), or any other symbol that represents nourishment or care, such as the Rune Berkana/Beork.

In practice, the Pagan and Wiccan community views as Kitchen Witches that small number of individuals who are visibly responsible for food preparation and service at an event of more than a few people. Most of our brothers and sisters will never notice (more on this later) the person who spotted the great deal at the farmers' market and brought a huge contribution for feast. Most will never notice or comment on produce brought from your garden or farm. They will not care where the meat came from; or that you got up at 4 AM in the freezing cold to stalk an animal, then wept over its sacrifice that your people might eat. If any of these contributions are ever acknowledged, it is only because the publicly acknowledged Kitchen Witch states it loudly as an announcement prior to letting anyone eat. As a Kitchen Witch, it becomes your responsibility to give this credit where it is due. It is possible to make great food with some ingredients that are less than top rate, thus the magic of the Kitchen Witch, but it is important to acknowledge the gifts and sacrifices of other people. Pointing out that the sauce is so d*mn good because of the fresh tomatoes is your duty, and your honor. In dishes I have prepared, homemade cheese and fresh herbs have improved Italian dishes, homegrown peppers and very scary home brewed hot sauces have made chilli that was average into something very special (that etched the spoon I was stirring it with).

A Kitchen Witch is a great social force in the community, even if they would choose not to be. Feeding someone in any way, physical or spiritual, is a direct route to their respect and affection. Because of this, a Kitchen Witch can create and enforce social rules if they choose to. As an example, I am one of the kitchen witches who works by the Rule "The help eats first." Anyone who chopped an onion, stirred a pot, or washed a dish in my kitchen gets to go to the head of the line and eat before everybody who didn't. The biblical phrase is "do not bind the mouth of the kine who tread the grain." Now, me personally, people will help me in the kitchen for hours at a time because my nervous breakdown and screaming after 10 hours or so cooking is very entertaining, and a great vocabulary lesson for people wanting to learn English vernacular. But for most of the rest of the Kitchen Witches out there, let me say it is very motivating to people not that they get to eat first, but that they are allowed an opportunity to see and sample a dish they helped prepare. You may feel that it is important to serve elders, children, or special needs individuals before the rest of the community (when I say "elders," I don't mean someone with a title, I mean someone not as young as they used to be). Perhaps your rule is that permanent feast gear eats before disposable. As a Kitchen Witch, this sort of decision should fall within your prerogatives. Oh, and in my part of the valley, we bless the food and pray before we eat, and anyone who has a problem with that can get the back part of my ring hand.

Blessed Be,

P. B. Owl

Blessing the Food

Food and drink is blessed ritually throughout the Pagan community, as well as throughout most other religious groups of all kinds. Much like Christian Communion, Cup and Cakes are blessed as part of ritual by most modern Pagans and Wiccans. This usually begins with the blessing of the cup with an athame (ritual knife), causing this part of the ritual to be referred to as "Chalice and Blade," which is the Great Rite (the union of God and Goddess) in symbol. Then the cakes are blessed. A portion is left over, ritually reserved for the Lord and Lady, consecrated to Them, and put in a special place, usually outdoors. A blessing for a meal will not always have Cup and Cake blessings, per se, but the prayer blessing the food will almost always acknowledge that the food comes from the Lord and Lady, and again, a ritual portion will be put aside. At Samhain it is common for a portion to be put aside for the ancestors, at Beltane, for the Fey. Sometimes a special dish is used, but even if it is not we commonly refer to the portion put aside for the God and Goddess as "The Lady's Plate." (We are a Goddess oriented religion, at least in part.) There are Cup blessings, cake blessings, and general blessings for food written and collected by many of our authors (including the author of what you are currently reading).

Sample Blessing

Lord and Lady, we Your children thank you for this food. We thank You for our lives, and this time we are able to spend together. We return to You this token, as a symbol that all of our nourishment, physical and spiritual, comes from You. We ask for Your Blessing, an it harm none and is for the good of all. So Mote It Be.

The Kitchen Witch Ten Commandments

(this section is suitable for posting in sacred kitchens)

I. Thou Shalt Not Let the People Go Hungry

II. Unless They are Being Jerks, in Which Case They Can Go to McDonald's (stolen and paraphrased fair and square from Kitchen Witches in Middle Tennessee)

III. Thou Shalt Not Serve the Food Late

IV. Unless the Stove and Oven You were Told Worked Just Fine, Don't in Fact, Work Just Fine

V. Thou Shalt Ask for Enough Help Nicely

VI. The First Time. Then Thou Shalt Scream and Use Bad Words Until You Get Enough Help

VII. Thou Shalt Make Enough Food (See the First Commandment)

VIII. Thou Shalt Serve the Food at the Right Temperature (Hint, Most Soups Should be Hot, Ice Cream is Supposed to be Cold)

IX. Thou Shalt Not Try to be Kitchen Witch and Anything Else Complicated, Like Gathering Coordinator (This Means You, Lady Rhiannon)

X. All Food Tastes Better When Made with Love

General Etiquette Toward the Kitchen and Kitchen Witch
(or, how to look like you've been to town before)

This section can be copied and displayed at Kitchens or listed online, in flyers and handouts as a set of Rules provided P. B. Owl and BlackWyrm Publications are cited *(which I just did).*

Dietary Restrictions

Never assume, unless you have made arrangements in advance, that the Kitchen Witch can accommodate your special dietary needs or restrictions. For best results, make sure this information gets to the Kitchen Witch as early as is possible. This means days or weeks, not going to the kitchen when you get to the gathering. Don't complain if your dietary restrictions haven't been accounted for unless you have made these arrangements and can prove it. Without documentation, it never happened. Do not eat the food specially made and designated for people with restrictive dietary needs you don't have until it is confirmed they have gotten enough. Putting a large piece of the vegetarian lasagna on your plate next to the meat sauce lasagna is fine only after the vegetarians have been served. (Real example.) Do not make the mistake of believing that your wants are as important as other people's needs. The fact you don't like onions and won't eat them is your issue, not that of the Kitchen Witch, necessarily. The fact that someone will go into anaphylactic shock and possibly die if they consume even trace amounts of shellfish is most definitely the business of the Kitchen Witch and the Medical Staff for the gathering. (This information should have been communicated to Registration as well, as this is the department that coordinates information.)

Preparation

Never bring food that has to be extensively prepared as a donation without arranging this ahead of time with the Kitchen Witch. Don't assume that space can be made for you to finish the dish in the on site kitchen unless this has been pre arranged. If you bring a premade dish, please bring a card with an ingredients list firmly fixed to the serving pan. If you can, make an effort to find out in advance what the needs/requests/planned menus of the Kitchen Witch are. Do not complain about the way in which a Kitchen Witch chooses to use your contribution, unless the contribution was not served at feast but went home with someone else after the gathering. This would be a complaint for the gathering coordinator. Do not unwrap, open, or sample food before the meal unless invited to do so (which happens to me all the time because other Kitchen Witches ask me to taste things and give seasoning suggestions). Many of us have special rituals, including prayer, to consecrate the food before the meal; it is disrespectful and rude to take the magic and mystery of this away from people who have worked hard to prepare a meal for you.

Share

Do not get in line for seconds until everyone has had firsts. Do not take extremely large portions of anything until everyone has been served (taking second and third helpings at the same time you take your first helping). Not only is this disrespectful and rude, it is very likely you will have overestimated either your appetite or your taste for a particular dish (remember, many Kitchen Witches are very upset by waste). Do not complain about pre measured portions sizes of some dishes as long as there is enough food to eat.

Keep Out

Do not enter the Kitchen unless dropping off a contribution, asking a legitimate, time sensitive question about the feast, or have been invited in by the Kitchen Witch. (I've been thinking about instituting a rule that says when you enter the Kitchen without an invitation you have to put a dollar in a penalty jar, and if the Kitchen Witch agrees it was a good reason you get 50 cents back.) Never, ever season a dish, add water or other liquids, or change the heat settings on any dish without the express direction and approval of the Kitchen Witch preparing it. Keep all non Kitchen related drama out of the Kitchen, and out of the way of the Kitchen Witch (easily identified as the person holding the big, sharp knife).

Tricks

These are exactly as advertised, tricks you pick up after over 15 years of trying to provide good food for large numbers of people at one time and on a limited budget.

Kitchen Tricks

Kitchen Zen

Proper time management and environment management will make your life as a Kitchen Witch easier and will always help with the quality of the food you prepare. Always allow for more time than you think you will need, especially if you are increasing a dish from family size to family reunion size for the first time. If you have down time, straighten up as you go. Throw away disposable items as they are used, clean counters whenever they have been used, and clean all pans, utensils, or other kitchen tools as quickly as possible. (It always takes less time to clean just used kitchen tools than if you wait as little as an hour for the food residue to set up on the plate, bowl, or glass.) Managing your time and environment is a form of Feng Shui; you will cook better food when you are not stressed and your environment is orderly, not chaotic.

ABC - Always Be Cooking

If you have access to the kitchen at the Gathering, and you are the Kitchen Witch, if there isn't at least one pot cooking on the stove or at least one pan baking in the oven, you are probably practising poor time management. Also, as a purely psychological tool for yourself and for others, it is reassuring to go to the kitchen and see or smell food cooking. When in doubt, bake potatoes, boil eggs, or put together a soup with stuff in it.

Breaking Bad

Knowing how to cook, knowing how to reset the breakers for the electricity, knowing how to turn on and turn off the primary water main, and knowing how to change the propane on the gas powered stove or griddle...are almost never overlapping skill sets. Plan accordingly, or suffer the wrath of Murphy (and whiny people).

Tools

Having the right tool for the right job is at least as important in the kitchen as it is in any other room in the house.

Knives

Dull knives hurt a lot more people than sharp knives.

Instructions

Never use a new kitchen tool, but especially a new electrical or motorized tool, without either reading the instruction manual or having a skilled user as an instructor. Both would be even better, if you can manage it.

Clothing

It is just barely possible to prepare dinner for 4 and not get stains on your clothes. It is completely impossible to prepare dinner for 40 and not get stains on your clothes. If you can use aprons, fine. I always wind up getting them caught on things. So, when cooking for large groups, I wear older clothes that I don't mind staining (black hides a lot of food stains, too).

Experiment Carefully

Don't ruin a meal for 100 people because your new pet cooking theory turns out to be cr*p. Having said this, try mixing one part soy sauce to one part strawberry jelly as a cooking sauce for Asian style beef dishes. Crazy good.

People Tricks

Can't Please 'em All

If you listen to the received cooking wisdom of the community and attempt to make a dish everyone will like, you will make a dish almost no one will like. Instead, either choose a short, well publicized menu that you know will not please everyone ("the flyer told you what we were having, too bad, so sad") or try for a larger number of dishes that take into account a majority of tastes and dietary restrictions (and you will still have menu complaints).

Critics

Ignore any criticism of the food that does not help you to improve the food. Always be able and willing to tell the difference between constructive, measured criticism and personal attacks motivated by irrational or self serving reasons. Always try to learn from every comment, even if what you learn is the patience not to dump a pot of boiling water over the head of someone who obviously knows a lot less about cooking than you do.

Hey, Go Get Me a...

If you have to delegate a task, be as specific as possible. Never assume that the person you are sending to the store knows there is a difference between yellow hot dog mustard and Dijon style mustard, or which one you want.

Health Tricks

Allergies

Food sensitivities and allergies are a pain in the butt, but also can stretch your skills as a cook and Kitchen Witch. I've done Atkins friendly dishes on request, made chili without onions or chili powder, made spaghetti without garlic or mushrooms, and modified my beloved, fairly stolen meatball recipe for one of my closest friends by removing the cheese crackers and substituting oats (gluten allergy). Here is a partial list of the food sensitivities and allergies I have personally encountered as a Kitchen Witch, i.e., every one of these things can make someone sick or kill them. Watermelon (that's mine). Shellfish. Onion. Garlic. Tomato. Chili pepper. Chocolate. Strawberry. Dairy (some of these are lactose intolerant and can use aged dairy products like cheese, or products made from goats' milk). Grapefruit. Pomegranate. Mustard (one of less than 40 people on Earth with an anaphylactic reaction to mustard attends Pagan gatherings in East Tennessee). Iron (no kidding, there is a community member who can't eat anything made in an iron skillet, it makes them really sick). Mushroom. Cranberry. Wheat. Soy. MSG (and if they can't have soy at all, they absolutely can't have MSG). Processed sugar. Honey (no child under two years old should be given honey, especially raw honey).

Ingredient Safety

Mature, responsible adults (there are a few in the Pagan community) need to be able to ask what ingredients are in a dish in order to avoid allergies or anaphylaxis. If you will be present the whole of service and have all the information in your head, fine, but I will guarantee the 3 minute period you take to have your only bathroom break in a 5 hour time span is exactly when someone will need the information. Clearly printed 3 by 5 cards of ingredient lists are a great thing, and should be kept with any leftovers (because watermelon makes me violently sick).

Food First Aid

Always have emergency food available. Small cans of orange juice in your fridge can provide immediate support for a diabetic, or tenderize/flavor a cut of meat that otherwise you won't be able to cut with a chainsaw. Sports drinks and bananas are good for muscle cramps, over exertion, and dehydration. Small packages of nuts, string cheese, a handy jar of peanut butter, or already cooked lean meat not only fixes a hypoglycemic attack quicker than anything else, but also grounds a ritual practitioner from luminal state/magical reality quicker than anything else. For the hypoglycemics, an apple added to the cheese is a big help towards recovery. If you think you are under psychic attack "First, eat a damn sandwich." – Seraphel of WynDragon. (Dion Fortune says it, too, in **Psychic Self Defense**, but Seraphel's version is much cooler). Most campers know that adding bleach (Clorox) to water at about one part in ten disinfects dishes and cleans your hands. What you may not know is if you are cooking and get a knife cut that bleach not only disinfects the wound, it will also help it close. (And it will sting like the dickens.)

Ingredient Tricks

Whatchamacallit

If you don't know how to use the ingredient, ask for help. Get good at recognizing real cooks from bad cooks who bullsh*t.

Meat

Don't be "married" to one type or cut of meat. Ground turkey or ground pork sausage are frequently a lot cheaper than ground beef. Turkey "ham" is a lot cheaper than ham, as is turkey "bacon" compared to pork bacon. Mackerel is a lot cheaper than salmon, and for some dishes, such as cooked patties, preferred by some people (I'm one of them). In the US, dark meat poultry cuts are almost always cheaper than white meat. Non traditional cuts and organ meats are frequently very affordable. At this writing, in my area, beef stew meat (from chuck roast) sells for $5/lb and whole fresh chicken livers for no more than $1.60/lb, frequently on an even better sale. Beef heart is running about the same, and cooks up like a pot roast or shoulder cut. Heart also works very well as ground meat. Also, give game meats a chance, many people have preferences for game meats over domestic animals if given a choice and the exposure. Ground venison (deer meat) was used in the best chili I ever had. Barbecued rabbit, southern style, slow smoked and slathered in a sweet, sticky sauce, is fantastic. I have never eaten duck that I didn't like, and here in the Southeastern US it is not uncommon for it to be served at Thanksgiving dinner. An extra note; in general, like pork, most large game meats (buffalo, bear, elk, venison) need to be thoroughly cooked, never served rare, and held at temperature for an extended period of time. This is done to avoid trichinosis and other food born illnesses.

Meat-ectomy

The most common mistake non vegetarians make when converting a conventional (with meat) recipe to a vegetarian version is to change it solely by removing this ingredient from a tested recipe and then being surprised when the flavor or texture is "off." Meat is a flavor enhancer that also adds bulk and texture. In a modern Western dish, it adds a lot of the bulk. Always test the vegetarian version for texture and flavor. Marinara sauces (Italian vegetarian tomato based "red" sauces) traditionally use chunkier cuts of vegetables and more varieties of vegetables than a classic red meat sauce (notably zucchini and bell pepper). One trick I have used is to remove the meat from the spaghetti sauce recipe and replace it with matchstick cut carrots, yellow "crookneck" squash, and zucchini to add texture and depth of flavor. And when I say matchstick, that is what I mean, if you use a fancy julienne cut for this you won't get the same texture. (Cook the carrots longer for uniform texture if you want to.) Add bulk to soups without meat by adding pasta or grain. Since many processed meats are spiced and salted, you may need to add additional seasoning when the dish becomes vegetarian. Personally, I suggest tarragon, "the little dragon," as it adds great depth of flavor and a certain "meatiness" hard to achieve without using meat or mushrooms (please see the section on food sensitivities and allergies). Another talented cook I know suggests another not terribly well known herb – grains of paradise – a well known natural flavor enhancer. Soy sauces and teriyaki sauces are as traditional for vegetarian options as they are for meat dishes. As a Kitchen Witch in the Pagan and Wiccan community these cooking issues are ones you will encounter at almost every event, as vegetarians make up between 5 to 10% of our attendees, and are very vocal about their food requirements. A note on vegetarian "meat." With the exception of TVP and some other dried soy preparations, I have found the premade vegetarian "burgers," "bacon," "sausage," etc., to be problematic. They tend to be very expensive per serving, don't taste particularly good even if you really like vegetables, and are shockingly high in artificial ingredients and preservatives. I was on a diet that restricted phosphates/phosphoric acid and was not able to eat a lot of processed or cured meats, so I looked into the vegetarian alternatives. It amazed me to find out that vegetarian bacon used more phosphates and nitrates than the real stuff made with pork.

Mad Cow

In any recipe that calls for ground beef and is strongly seasoned (spaghetti, meatballs, lasagna, chili, sloppy joes), use 1/3 of that amount in ground beef and 1/3 of that amount in pork sausage. By many people's taste it will actually taste better, and the cost is reduced about 50%. Most people will never notice any reduction in the amount of meat. The same trick can be done by adding TVP instead of sausage for the same level of savings. You will not increase flavor, as with the sausage, but you do reduce a lot of the fat.

Protein

Anecdote from dealing with vegetarians – TVP (textured vegetable protein) is the dried, small piece soy protein product, that when rehydrated, gives protein, texture, and bulk to vegetarian dishes. What it does not give is a lot of flavor. I was introduced to TVP in spaghetti over 30 years ago, and have cooked with it successfully in lasagna and chili, dishes that can rely on spices and other ingredients for a lot of flavor. Because it does not have a lot of flavor of its own, one trick is to rehydrate the TVP in the liquid you will be cooking in, which for all of the dishes I have mentioned is tomato juice or tomato sauce. Here begins the tale of me getting yelled at for no good reason. I was rehydrating the TVP in a bowl of tomato juice on my kitchen counter when the crazy vegetarian (a frequently redundant statement in my experience, even for some of the ones I love dearly) comes into the kitchen and screams, "You're trying to feed me meat and kill me!" I responded, "Smell it." "What?!?" "Smell it." "Umm, that doesn't smell like meat, what is it?" "Dried soy protein rehydrating in tomato juice; if I wanted to kill you I wouldn't use meat, I'd use one of these big, sharp, knives. Now get out of my kitchen." TVP, also referred to as TSP (textured soy protein), soy flakes, and soy chips, is a great staple to have on hand even if you are not vegetarian. Shelf stable if stored in an airtight container at normal room temperature, TVP is great for long term back up protein, like a jar of peanut butter. Pound for pound, when rehydrated, it costs about half the cost of ground meat with almost no fat. When added to noodles or rice, the amino acids make a complete protein. Larger varieties are sold as "soy crumbles." Using TVP in a spaghetti sauce or similar preparation will speed time to table if you otherwise had to thaw meat, even in a microwave.

Something's Fishy

Fresh, raw fish that smells "fishy" is fishy. It is probably going bad, and is not safe to eat. See above rule, there are a few stronger smelling fish, check with someone who knows better, if they really do. Seriously, you have to learn who is full of bullsh*t.

Meat Flavoring

Remember, when working with a limited budget and feeding large numbers of people, that meat is traditionally a flavoring and not a main ingredient. If you are trying to provide protein to large numbers of people then eggs, cheese, soy, and some nuts are much less expensive. You can also mix grains and pulses (red beans and rice, pinto beans and cornbread). Some dishes combine a little meat with grains and pulses (jambalaya, dirty rice, gumbo). The traditional boiled Irish dinner starts with the smallest corned beef brisket you can find at the store, your largest cooking pot, and cabbage and potatoes to fill it (you could also use carrots, rutabagas, parsnips and/or turnips if you are either communist or English). Serve with fresh pones of corn bread or loaves of soda bread to soak up the potlikker. Remember, good fresh butter will make the bread even better.

Noodling Around

Thick noodle, thin sauce. Thin noodle, thick sauce. (Which sounds dirty.)

The thicker the noodle, the longer the cooking time. (Which also sounds dirty.)

Use Your Noodle

Unless served in a baked dish, such as lasagna, noodles are really tricky in large amounts (so is rice). For best results, remember that noodles in large quantities continue to cook after being taken off the heat source unless immediately shocked in cold water. Noodles can be taken off the heat 2 minutes before perfect consistency, dumped into clean ice chests (plastic only, no Styrofoam or metal), and lightly coated with olive oil to prevent clumping. If appropriate for the dish, think about using small or thin noodles as this can reduce the cooking time by up to 40% (just look at the suggested cooking times on a package of spaghetti noodles as compared to those on a pack of angel hair pasta).

Soup Grains

Don't have time to cook down grain in a soup? Use instant rice or use orzo and other very small quick cooking pastas. Instant potato flakes thicken a soup or stew quickly as well.

Shrooms

In any recipe that calls for beef and mushrooms (spaghetti, beef stroganoff), cut the amount of beef in half and double or even triple the amount of mushrooms. Most people will never think the dish lacks meat, and the cost is reduced by about 50%.

In a dish where canned mushrooms are used in a cooked down sauce or casserole, always purchase "pieces and stems" as opposed to "whole" or "caps." This saves you at least 40% on the cost of this ingredient.

Powders

Instant cake mixes, corn muffin mixes, pancake mixes, and biscuit mixes are your friends. So are instant mashed potatoes. And in certain circumstances, all of these things can be substituted for each other. (And if you don't like potato cakes, you are a bad person of dubious character.)

Bread Spread

Bread is almost always better with butter, gravy, honey, jelly, jam, Karo syrup, or molasses. Bread is almost never better served with margarine, but a few bread and biscuit recipes made with margarine are surprisingly good.

Dressing

A salad dressing can be made from almost any kind of oil combined with almost any kind of vinegar. I served a 3 bean and pasta salad with a dressing made from vegetable cooking oil and balsamic vinegar and it got compliments.

Inventory Tricks

Me, Myself, and I

Consider the possibilities of DIY. A whole pork belly costs a fraction of what bacon does, and allows you to cure your own with the exact spices, salt level, and thickness of cut. We bought some "thick cut" bacon recently, and my response after opening the package was "If this is thick cut, I would d*mn sure hate to see thin cut." Waste and costs can be reduced for gatherings and Sabbats by using preservation methods such as canning, pickling, or freezing to keep and store "extra" contributions for future events. Always think about the idea of preparing ingredients or condiments as well as complete dishes. Combining oil, vinegar, and Italian seasoning mix is a lot cheaper sometimes than purchasing bottled Italian salad dressing.

Serving Sizes

Cutting items into suggested serving sizes is good. If in doubt of quantity on the main dish, serving out the item like a cafeteria lunch lady is better. If there are complaints, politely explain that individuals can come back for seconds when everyone has been served. Another way of controlling waste is to only bring out one platter, casserole dish, individual turkey, etc., at one time, before bringing out the next one.

Shop Smart

Always use price per pound or ounce labels where provided to get true cost. Never assume the bigger can is the better deal, or that the generic is cheaper than the name brand.

If you can, before purchasing, compare prices at multiple stores.

Brand Names

Concerning brands and brand names, make sure you are not just paying for a name if you don't need to. But, sometimes a famous branded product is famous for a reason besides good advertising. I have a favorite brand of ketchup, not because of flavor particularly, but because of consistency (it is almost never too watery or too stiff). I have a favorite brand of yellow mustard, because of its flavor. I have a favorite mayonnaise and a favorite whipped salad dressing (if you're not from the South, "salad dressing" doesn't just mean something for lettuce, but refers to a product similar to mayonnaise used for sandwiches, fruit salads, potato salad, and cole slaw. Remember as well that your need or recipe can make a bug into a feature. My meatball recipe needs a cheap knockoff cheese cracker, made with a lot of shortening or oil. A crisp, light good quality cracker won't serve as a binder as well in the recipe, I've tried. In other goods, I buy jeans that don't have the rivets at all the pockets, because I do not in fact, herd cows, build houses, or do any of the other things that would cause seams to pop or pockets to tear off. And if you don't do any of those things, getting jeans with rivets means you're paying more for something that won't last you as long, because rivets beat the cr*p out of the jeans in the washer and dryer. Again, just be sure you are paying for your need, not a name.

Right Size

In a fixed price ($1 or 99 cent) store, look for these things: Greatest quantity, pounds, ounces, etc. Luxury items you might otherwise not be able to afford. New items you might not otherwise try. Small quantities of things like spices that you would otherwise buy in larger bulk in a standard store, but that you only need the ingredient for one meal (even though the meal is a large one).

Industrial Size

When cooking for 20 or more, even if not shopping a large quantity outlet store specializing in industrial sizes, even the average grocery store will have at least a small section of industrial size cans of things like spaghetti sauce, vegetables, and premade pasta like ravioli that you should check first. For the home cook, these portions are usually too big to be a bargain due to the potential for waste and spoilage, but for a gathering, some of these are the most cost effective. As always, check the price per ounce or pound and compare to smaller sized containers of the same item. If you can't find this section in your grocery store (and in my closest grocery store it is a very small section of fewer than 20 items), ask a clerk or stocker.

Leftovers

Where do leftover bits go? Soup is a good place, so are casseroles or "hot dish," depending on where you are from. Hash is a good choice, and there are always sandwiches. But, if you like them, and are any good at preparing them, the ultimate garbage disposal food is an omelet. You get rid of prechopped vegetables, you get rid of leftover cooked meat. You have a use for a small amount of an ingredient that would otherwise go to waste. It gives both flavor and interest to eggs, which some people find rather boring, and stretches the eggs you have to make more portions and feed more people. Not confident in your omelet skills? Buy pre made pastry crusts, scramble the eggs in a bowl, fold in the ingredients, pour into the pastry shell. Cook in the oven for 15-20 minutes at 350 or until lightly browned and cooked throughout the quiche. In both cases, be sure the ingredients are chopped fine, as the texture can be unpleasant otherwise and the bigger pieces don't cook well and can be cold when served. One of the worst things I was ever served at a gathering was supposed to be a broccoli omelet, and the pieces of broccoli were the size of the fork, giving the dish an unpleasant texture (and the broccoli was cold).

Use What You've Got

If you have potatoes, use potatoes. If you have onions, use onions (see recipes). If you have eggs, use eggs. Not preparing enough food is embarrassing, and makes you look stupid. Not preparing enough food when there was plenty of food to prepare is extremely embarrassing and shows a bunch of people that yes, in fact, you are really stupid.

Example: Knowing I was doing an Italian meal for feast at a gathering, one attendee brought me a big bunch of fresh fennel. If you don't know it, fennel, especially fennel seed, is an ingredient a lot of people put in Italian red sauces. Personally, I'm not a big fan, especially of the seeds. But you use what you've got; I had this huge bunch of fresh herbs, I had olive oil (duh, Italian meal)), and garlic (double duh), as well as other spices and loaves of crusty bread. So the dry ingredients listed (except the bread) were chopped fine, spices were added (basil, oregano, black pepper) and presto....pesto. OK, "normal" pesto uses fresh basil and pine nuts as the base. Nobody who ate the "fake" pesto complained about it. The person who brought the fennel felt their contribution had been respected, and one guy had an epiphany that at first looked like a stroke. "You can *make* pesto? I've been paying 5 bucks for a little bitty jar of this stuff, and this tastes *better!*"

The Incredible Bulk

Another trick about large amounts: If you are not used to preparing larger quantities, you need to make sure all raw animal products (including eggs) have enough cooking time and are cooked safely and thoroughly. Exceptional quality fish is safe raw (and if you are no judge of this, do not try to do it). Excellent quality beef is safe at medium rare (reddish in the middle but hot throughout); good quality beef is safe at medium (pink in the middle). Pork, chicken, and eggs need to be cooked thoroughly, as should all wild game and offal of any variety.

One more thing about large amounts: The extra time required for prepping and cooking food is a lot more than you would think unless you have done a lot of it. If you are taking a dish for a family of 5 and making enough for 20, it really can take almost 4 times as long.

Liquid Tricks

Cuppa Joe

Never, ever run out of coffee. People will do without a lot of things. Dinner can be late, some dishes can run out. Even if you run out of sugar or creamer, you may be forgiven, but people get downright hateful if you run out of coffee.

A Merry Spirit

Never cook with an alcoholic product you wouldn't serve or drink. Yes, this means if a recipe calls for wine and you never drink wine, cook something else, because you won't have a good idea of what the finished dish should taste like. Primarily it means don't use the cheap stuff if you only drink the good stuff, and never ever use "cooking wine" or "cooking sherry." You're better off with "processed cheese food product" or "fruit drink with artificial flavors added." In all seriousness, for large events (20 or more) where you don't know all the attendees well, consider forgoing the use of alcohol in the food altogether. Many in our community are in recovery, and even the taste of alcohol with all the actual alcohol cooked out, can be enough to trigger a relapse. This is why many rituals offer a non alcoholic Cup only, or a choice of two cups. This vulnerability in our extended family by choice is also the only reason I would ever suggest using an artificial vanilla flavoring.

Taters Gonna Tate

A trick so old it is almost forgotten: If any liquid based dish (especially a soup) is too salty, put in a raw potato for several minutes and this will leech out some of the salt. The potato can be used for another dish (and has already been salted).

The Gravy Train

Brown gravy mix will cover a multitude of culinary sins. So will chocolate sauce.

Affordable Foods People Make Fun of to Feed Large Groups

Bologna (Baloney)

A sandwich filling of the US childhood, bologna can be used in a lot of ways that some people actually like as grown ups. (As a sandwich the correct recipe is one slice thick cut bologna, one slice American cheese, with Kraft Miracle Whip Salad Dressing on two pieces of white bread. All other choices are wrong.) If you were raised at least middle class, and especially if you are younger than 35, you may not know that bologna is fried for several recipes. Very thin slices of bologna cut into strips are crisp fried and used as a substitute for bacon. If you fry whole slices of bologna and do not vent or cut it like you would a pie crust, it will rise up at the edges, forming a bowl or cup. The traditional recipe for making this a feature and not a "bug" is to fill the cup with a variety of ingredients. The kind that used to be served in public schools was mashed potatoes, green peas on top of the potatoes, and then covered with grated cheese. If you are low brow enough in your tastes to like this, you might also try the cups filled with macaroni and cheese. For a Kitchen Witch, the fool proof serving size on these is part of the upside. Personally, I'm peasant enough that one of my favorites is to take the smaller roll of uncut chub bologna called cracker bologna, slice it thick, and eat it cold on, you guessed it, crackers. I'm for saltines; you can choose something fancier if you like.

Canned Tuna

Yes, we all remember tuna salad sandwiches from brown bag lunches, and many of us like tuna salad, as weight or health conscious adults, served on tomato wedges. Mock it if you want to, but tuna casserole, either made from a box or with your own starch base and sauce of your choice, is cheap, easy, and fast. Since the tuna is already cooked, this is one animal product where the cooking time is not a safety issue. One standard 6 oz can is the protein for 2-3 servings of casserole.

Spam

Don't b*tch about Spam (from Hormel Foods) until you've had Treet (from Armour Star). Works pretty well a couple of different ways. Like bologna, can be sliced very thin, and fried crispy to use as "fakon" (fake bacon). If you bake it in sauce, like a ham, draining off the grease, it isn't bad. It works well in BBQ sauce or typical ham glazes like soy sauce, brown sugar, orange juice, and pineapple. Spam is pork, if you treat it with a little TLC like you'd use on a more traditional cut of pork you might be favorably surprised with the results. Never, ever insult Spam in front of anyone from Hawaii, it is beloved comfort food there. You might as well make fun of a cheese steak sandwich in Philadelphia, or grits almost anywhere below the Mason-Dixon Line. Translation: you will get your *ss kicked.

Smoked Sausage/Kielbasa/Hot Dogs

Skin smoked sausage or kielbasa, chop it, and use it in a spaghetti sauce to cut cooking time since it is already cooked. This is Spaghetti Bolognase, and a lot of people like it as well or better than other meat sauce recipes. Small or cocktail sausages in sauce are a great appetizer, and fast to prepare as they are pre cooked. Hot dogs and even the other cased sausages are usually very affordable, and are now made of almost any meat or combination of meats you can think of.

Pork and Beans

OK, lots of us have had homemade baked beans that started life as white beans in a tomato sauce, before Aunt Begonia added molasses, barbecue sauce, ketchup, chopped onion, and strips of bacon on top. Depending on whose Aunt Begonia is doing the dish, it ranges from "meh" to pretty good, d*mn good when served next to hamburgers and hotdogs. But I'm a Kitchen Witch, and I'm trying to serve people food they will like, that will fill them up, meet a few of their nutritional needs, and still be affordable in the quantities we're talking about. Homemade beans and wieners is a great dish for this, winter or summer, the only difference is if you serve it hot or cold. Cut the hot dogs (smoked sausage, kielbasa, bratwurst, or whatever meat in casing was on sale) into small pieces and brown in skillet or the pot you're going to make the dish in. If serving cold, let the meat cool before adding beans. Add beans, heat if desired. Add in extra tomato sauce, ketchup or BBQ sauce if you like. Can add some Worcestershire sauce and/or hot sauce for "zip." A little black pepper will go a long way. If you choose to sweeten this at all, remember that you will be treading close to the baked beans line. Liked cooked pintos, cooked white or "pea" beans will get mushy very fast when cooked again, so heat only until hot and do not over stir. This is a great time to use a non stick pan. 6 ounces of beans and half of a standard hot dog (6 one half inch pieces) is a good serving size for an adult.

Canned Corn

This was Poppy's (my grandfather) favorite thing to cook on planet Earth, "Blackened Corn." Take a can of whole kernel corn. Drain it. Heat an iron skillet large enough that the corn will just coat the bottom of the skillet. Use large wads of bacon grease. (OK, if you're a sissy or a vegetarian you can use butter or oil, Poppy's words on that). Put frying liquid into pan, it should sizzle and smoke. Immediately put in corn, stir rapidly while adding salt and more black pepper than you've ever seen a human use at one time. Fry until corn is wrinkled and making popping sounds. Amazing with some Cajun seasoning, red pepper flakes, or a little chili powder added.

Peanut Butter

Shelf stable, high in protein, and convenient to use, if you grew up in the US you probably had peanut butter sandwiches (with jelly or banana) throughout childhood and possibly in adulthood. Peanut butter is inexpensive, and has multiple other uses. It is the cornerstone of many "no bake" cookie, candy, and fudge recipes. It is an excellent thickener, and in other parts of the world, ground peanuts are frequently added to soups, stews, and sauces of all kinds. Spicy peanut sauce is an Asian staple for dishes with noodles or rice.

Boxed Cake or Brownie Mix

Prepare mix per box instructions. Break up pieces of whatever candy bar you like or have sitting around. Pour mix into pan. Glob in spoonfuls of honey, jelly (strawberry is awesome in brownie mix), or peanut butter, stud top with candy bar pieces, cook per box instructions. Will frequently be as ugly as sin and taste amazing.

Instant Mashed Potatoes

A great thickener for stews or soups that works fast. Also, because of the smooth consistency, great for potato cakes if you have left overs. Stir an egg and flour into cold leftover potatoes until stiff, pat out into thin cakes. Fry at medium high heat in small amount of butter or oil until golden brown on each side. Can serve by themselves, with gravy, or with ketchup (my favorite). You can't leave these d*mn things unattended for an eye blink while cooking, or they will burn on you, smell NASTY, and taste worse. They are even better if you melted in some cheese while making the mashed potatoes.

Ramen Noodles

Millions of college students can't be wrong, right? Using as big a pot as you need, allow half a block ramen per person. Barely cover ramen with boiling water, cook for half a package time, usually 1 minute or so. The water will be almost entirely absorbed. Add to pan of stir fried vegetable and/or meat in the sauce and seasonings of your choice. When noodles are thoroughly stirred in (a minute or so), remove from heat and serve. Shockingly good, very cheap.

Canned Biscuits

Great for homemade pasties (meat pies). Be careful and don't over stuff the pocket, or the pie will tear. They work OK for homemade fried apple pie, too. Used as either a top or bottom layer to add breading to casseroles of various kinds There is no better "drop" dumpling for chicken and dumplings, as far as I am concerned, than torn pieces of canned biscuits dropped into simmering chicken stock filled with big pieces of chicken. (This works pretty well for fruit and dumpling desserts also, such as apples and dumplings or peaches and dumplings.)

Ten Things That Ruin Food at Gatherings

Lack of Support

This can be financial, equipment, or personnel lack. If you don't receive enough funds to purchase enough of the right food, and/or you don't receive enough food donations to feed the people you need to, then people will go hungry at worst, and at best be eating food that is boring or bad. If you don't have the right equipment, there are things you can't do. Now, most Kitchen Witches can improvise pretty d*mn well when we have to; this is a central element of our magic. But it is hard to improvise an oven or cook top; you can do it, but it isn't fast. (If you have to, you can improvise a stove top by heating pots directly on a fry grill, or on a grate over a fire. To fake an oven, you need either a dutch oven closed cooking dish with handle that hangs over a fire, or coals and a lot of aluminium foil. What I was always taught to call "scout packs," being a meat, vegetables, and a marinade, like Italian dressing, is wrapped in a foil pack and put under coals to heat for 2 to 3 hours. This same technique is good for hard vegetables like potatoes and corn on the cob.) It is barely possible for one person who is skilled, fast, and energetic to cook a meal for 20 by themselves if they have enough time and the right equipment. Above 20, this possibility drops. If you don't have enough help, both quantity and quality of the food will suffer.

Time Management Problems

The Kitchen Witch does not properly use time, and either food is undercooked or not enough food gets prepared for just this reason. Indirectly, poor time management results in stress for the Kitchen Witch and disorder in the kitchen. Time management issues are such a problem for gatherings (and not just in the kitchen), that even the appearance of these issues can cause backlash and complaints, even when they aren't really issues.

Poor Planning

You don't need to agonize over recipes forever, or take that long to figure out what to prepare. But you do need to look at the materials you have to work with, including the assistance of other people, and plan accordingly. A pad of paper to write down a menu plan or a "things to do" list is worth its weight in my meatballs (and my meatballs are a lot tastier than gold). Keeping track of time, including a realistic appraisal of what can be done in the time you have available, is key.

No One in Overall Charge of the Kitchen

You can have a kitchen run relatively smoothly with no overall "Head" Kitchen Witch in charge of all the meals at the event. After all, the night owl who didn't stop cooking until 11 PM is probably not going to be cooking breakfast at 5 AM. But, I have never seen a meal put together by multiple people work successfully unless someone was in charge of it. There needs to be someone on every meal who has the final say about what gets cooked and when. There needs to be a person to make quick decisions about the use of resources and time. Without this person, there is a huge potential for confusion and problems, and it just seems to produce unnecessary stress; most people are just political, or pack animal, enough that they can accept a designated authority figure for a task fairly well, but if one is not designated there is a lot of jostling of elbows and attempts to establish a pecking order. A big part of the issue with this is that it wastes time, and can result in lousy food.

Non-Kitchen Drama in the Kitchen, or Affecting the Kitchen

The 50 people who want to be fed dinner do not care that the Kitchen Witch didn't get enough help because he or she is on the Gathering Coordinator's personal sh*t list. People don't care that the two people running the kitchen are a mother and daughter fighting over one or the other's choice in companions or friends. At some events, depending on the time of day or night, the Kitchen Witch is the only authority figure that attendees can locate, making it easy for the Kitchen Witch to get drawn into Security, Registration, Vending, or Site issues that have nothing to do with the food or getting the food to the table. This can suck up time, focus, and mental energy that needed to be directed toward feeding people good tasting and nutritious food.

Too Many People in Charge of the Same Dish

Too many is defined as more than one. Sure, it is appropriate to ask an assistant to stir a dish, chop onions, or peel potatoes. But, if more than one person is seasoning a dish, or if people think that "someone else" is keeping track of how long the cake has been in the oven, you get bad food, burnt food, or undercooked food (which is the dangerous one). Any one dish needs its own Kitchen Witch, its very own "Mommy" or "Daddy" to take good care of it.

Cleanliness is Next to Godliness

Filthiness is next to trichinosis and salmonella: Clean every tool before you use it. Clean every tool after you use it. Clean as you go. Clean you as you go. Antibacterial soap and bleach water are your new best friends.

Unfamiliar Ingredients, Improperly Used

I've already said this, but it bears repeating. If you are using ingredients (or for that matter, kitchen tools) that you have never used before, you either need d*mn good instructions from a recipe, or advice from another cook familiar with the ingredient. These days, looking it up on the Internet is a pretty good idea, too, if you can get reception. Pagan Gatherings are notorious for being the worst places on earth for cell tower reception, and can make your smart phone look pretty stupid. However you get the information, get it, and be sure you can trust it.

Letting a Theme Get in the Way of Good Food or Good Service

Normally this starts with an idea or set of ideas that sound very good on paper, but are impractical in practice and are connected to some of the other mistakes on this list. It sounds great to make any Harvest festival a traditional American Thanksgiving meal; but in practice, roasting whole turkeys in camp ovens is very difficult, time consuming, and expensive. There are traditional foods for every Sabbat, and inexperienced Kitchen Witches try to serve traditional items they have never prepared before.

Forgetting that Feeding Our People is a Sacred Task that Honors the God(s)

I joke, and I curse. I get frustrated with setbacks based on equipment failure and volunteer help that forgets to show up. But I try very hard to remember always that this is a holy calling. I do this work because I see its benefits for my people, and it allows me to serve in a very direct and visceral way that is different from leading rituals, teaching classes, and writing books. A Kitchen Witch who forgets these things usually turns into an angry and overly controlling cook who produces bad or boring food in a stressful environment and an unsafe manner.

The Ten Weirdest Things I've Seen as a Kitchen Witch

A Man with an Axe (in the Kitchen)

Here are the consequences of timing and planning issues. There was an enormous block of frozen beef, it had to have weighed 50 lbs. It had not been given time to thaw, and 2 hours before serving it was a meatsicle 3 feet long. So, this guy goes over to the fire pit and gets the axe they've been using to chop wood, cleans it up a bit, and starts hitting this beef slab as hard as he can. Did I mention he didn't really warn anybody first before swinging a big frickin' axe in a tiny kitchen? Well, hunks of frozen beef got thrown on the grill and the meal got made, but axes swung near the light fixtures is a bad thing.

Dead Animals in the Freezer

No, not meat, because meat is the cleaned ready to use pieces of dead animals, not whole, with the fur and tail and eyeballs, dead animals. I've seen this literally dozens of times now, and it is still weird.

All the Available Kitchen Floor Space Covered in Potatoes

Tiny kitchen, I left for five minutes only. I came back and there was no way to get to the stove until I had someone move sacks of potatoes. A lot of sacks of potatoes.

Other People's Recipes

We all grow up eating certain things, based on where we live, cultural norms, and what our parents like to eat and/or cook. Depending on your cultural and socio-economic background, I am sure that some of the recipes and food suggestions included in this book range from pretty d*mn weird to downright revolting. The first time I sat down (over 30 years ago, how time flies) to a plate of spaghetti that used the largest noodles available, red pepper flakes in the sauce and "gasp" NO MUSHROOMS, I almost said "I thought we were having spaghetti?." Mixing one part barbecue sauce, one part teriyaki sauce, and one part grape jelly to use as baking sauce for cocktail wienies sounds weird when you first hear about it, but this has been a staple of family reunions throughout the Southeast for at least 40 years. Most "secret" ingredients sound pretty weird, mine included. I am the cook who puts cottage cheese and the little square cheese crackers in the meatballs, and sweet potato in the split pea soup. I've had chili where the beans were cooked in day old coffee (surprisingly good), a beer and cheese sauce poured over what is otherwise essentially a ham sandwich on toast (depends on who makes it and how good the ingredients are), and the standard beef cooked in red wine (good if cooked long enough, nasty tasting otherwise). Always be open to change, and try to recover from food prejudices (if you learn nothing else from this entire book, please learn this lesson). But, don't be afraid to consciously make the decision that you don't like a dish, and subsequently as the Head Kitchen Witch in Charge, you don't think a lot of other people will either. Remember however these two things; ham soaked in rum before baking is fantastic, and canned turkey and sauerkraut as toppings on one of the boxed pizza kits is crazy good.

Polenta

OK, there is nothing essentially weird about polenta, a corn meal dish popular in European cooking. But someone trying to cook and serve polenta for 500 hundred people under campground kitchen conditions... that was pretty strange.

A Three Feet by Two Feet Block of Noodles

If you don't follow the instructions in this book about how to prepare noodles for large groups of people and both overcook them even a little bit and don't use some oil to keep them from sticking together, your large pot or ice chest full of noodles will become one large block of noodles. My ice chest was three feet by two feet. We resorted to carving off slices, like you would with a meatloaf, pouring the sauce over it and trying to separate it on the plate for each serving. The dish didn't taste bad, but it was a peculiar looking presentation and I still think the texture was a little odd. (It didn't stop people from eating it, I will point out.)

A $500 Bag of Saffron Next to a 99¢ Bag of Potato Chips

Really.

Breaker Comedy

Turn on the radio, the fan goes out. Turn on the microwave, the radio goes out. Turn on the overhead light, the microwave goes out. Turn on the fan, the overhead light goes out.

A Naked Man Frying Things

Nudity happens at Pagan events. This is a given. But there are bits I value and do not want hot oil or grease to spatter on. So, I got a visceral sense of "bad plan, very bad plan" when I saw a man frying bacon while only wearing flip flops.

A Tiny Naked Woman on a Stool Reaching Up to a Pot on the Stove that was Still Too Tall for Her, Spanking the Beef Stew with a Paddle

I can't really add anything, that last sentence speaks for itself.

Recipes

OK, some these recipes are more like general outlines. Here's why. If you are already a talented (in your head, if not in the real world) cook or Kitchen Witch, you're just going to change the recipe anyway, even the first time you cook it. If you are inexperienced, or just plain bad at this, no matter how precise the instructions are you will screw them up the first few times. Hint: If you can't pour p*ss out of a boot with written directions on the heel, I'm talking to you right now. Not to mention that 375 on my oven may bear no resemblance whatsoever to 375 on your oven. (Translation, if you need to cook something longer, do it. Also, if you don't test them out on yourself and a small group of test subjects and guinea pigs before serving any of these dishes to large crowds, you deserve what you get.) So, these recipes are written in the same flowing, conversational style as the rest of these musings and meanderings. A "recipe" may contain several different variations clumped together for convenience and similarity of theme and/or preparation. Also, recipes for items intended to be used together tend to be listed together.

Onion Flowers

You will get a lot of donated onions, learn to cook with them. This recipe is a great place to start. Take onions and peel, cutting root end flat for cooking and presentation. From top to bottom, cut onion into eighths, but don't complete the cuts at the bottom. Pull each section apart, again without separating it from the base of the onion, giving it the appearance of a blooming flower. Dip into a slightly thinned cornbread or corn muffin mix (if the instructions give a recipe to dip corn dogs or onion rings, use that). For best results, fry in deep fryer until golden. Onions have a lot of moisture, stand well back and use eye protection. For less fat, you can try this baked variation. After dipping onions, place bottom down on pre greased cookie sheet. Sprinkle on panko crumbs or crushed croutons for extra crunch. Bake at 375 for 15 to 20 minutes or until onions are softened. If crust is not golden brown, use broiler setting for 2 to 3 minutes. You can season either variety with salt, pepper, Parmesan cheese, and/or Cajun seasoning. Allow 1 onion per person if using as a side dish, can split one onion between two people if using as an appetizer. Serve with ketchup, blue cheese dressing, or spicy aioli.

Spicy Aioli for Onion Flowers

OK, aioli is the fancy word people use when they don't want to say either "mayonnaise" or "mayonnaise with other stuff in it." It doesn't make this a bad dipping sauce, it just makes it a good dipping sauce with a stupid name. Per whole onion to be served, take two tablespoons of mayonnaise. Add one chipotle pepper, either dried and rehydrated or preserved in oil, and chop very fine in a food processor or by hand (if the grind isn't fine enough, the texture of the aioli will be gritty). Combine into mayonnaise with one teaspoon of Worcestershire sauce, with garlic and black pepper to taste. Spicy, but not overwhelming.

Baked Onions, Asian Style

While we're talking about onions; Once Upon A Time, a very large gathering with lots of people had not gotten enough food donations. Except for onions. There were 200 lbs of onions. So, the Kitchen Witch had the onions rinsed, but not peeled, and the tops sliced off (it didn't take an hour for 200 lbs of onions). Then, soy sauce, which was also present in gallons, was poured on every onion, liberally. The onions were then baked in the skins for 45 minutes at 350, covered for the first 20 minutes and hit with soy sauce again. This is freaking delicious. Try it with one onion at home. Allow approximately one onion per person.

Rice Balls

While I'm on an Asian theme, let's talk about rice and rice balls. Rice, like onions and potatoes, is an inexpensive bulk ingredient that either the Kitchen Witch might find for a great bargain price, or somebody else might and bring it as a contribution. I believe that your best bet for cooking rice is a rice cooker, because it turns off when finished cooking and then keep the rice warm. In any case, Japanese style rice balls, onigiri, are a great, cheap, easy side dish, service presentation, or snack. First cook rice with a heavy admixture of rice wine vinegar and white sugar, using it to replace about one quarter of the suggested amount of water. Let rice cool. When rice can be handled, form into balls, and roll in furikake until thoroughly coated. Furikake is a Japanese seasoning mix available in any Asian speciality market selling Japanese products. The basic ingredients are usually sesame seeds, seaweed, and salt. Other ingredients such as fish flakes, egg, pepper, sugar, and MSG are used in the different varieties of furikake. Serve balls at room temperature. Can use soy sauce, teriyaki sauce, or just about any leftover Chinese restaurant sauce packets to flavor. Great with any Japanese main dish.

Potato Soup

You are going to get potatoes donated to the kitchen, learn to cook with them. Peel potatoes, removing "eyes" (little root growths) or bad spots. The reason for peeling the potatoes is not just aesthetic; bad spots or green spots are not very visible under the peel, and just one or two bad potatoes can throw the flavor of an entire dish "off." With a normal size all purpose/baking potato cut in half and the quarter each half, at least. For soup you don't want pieces much larger than two inches by one inch, partly because it unnecessarily increases the cooking time. Put potatoes in pot, cover with water, adding some extra (you can always pour off water). If you need to reduce the time for cooking, you can start with boiling water. For a simple "cream of potato" soup, after potatoes have cooked until soft but not falling apart, add milk, half and half, cream, or condensed milk – whatever you have handy. This is definitely a dish where "fat equals flavor," and the richer the dairy product you use, the creamier and richer the soup will be. Add butter. Add more butter. If you're serving it to me, add some more butter. Season with salt and black pepper to taste. If you're serving it to me, add more pepper. Can add finely grated cheese, especially as a bowl garnish when serving (if you put it in the pot you risk the cheese sticking and burning on the bottom. Good garnished with chives, the tops of green onions, or Parmesan cheese. For a Vegan version use no dairy products and thicken with instant mashed potato flakes, can use vegetable broth for additional depth of flavor. Either of these versions benefits from the addition of some chopped, pre fried onion or garlic pieces. For meat eaters, small bits of ham or bacon are a great addition as well. Like the onions and garlic, pre fry the ham or bacon before adding it to the soup. Personally, I don't like crackers in potato soup, but I won't tell people about your secret shame if you don't.

Homemade Vegetable Broth

Use chopped pieces of carrot, celery and onion (mirepoix, if you're being French and fancy). Add any other fresh vegetable ends and clean peelings you choose, like broccoli stems and outside cabbage leaves. Cook until all vegetables are soft, strain out solids. Preseason to taste if desired. Use as a base for soups, or as a fortified cooking liquid for almost any vegetable dish.

Stew

Brown cubes or chunks of stew meat (usually from chuck roast if beef). Any red meat works well for this, as does pork and mutton. The best stew I've ever eaten was lamb stew in an Irish pub and grub. When meat is seared, add onions and quickly stir. Add cooking liquid, usually water. Can add red wine, steak sauce, Worcestershire sauce, or beef stock later in cooking if you want to. Usually made with carrots and potatoes, cut into pieces. Cook carrots a little longer than the potatoes, unless you like your carrots firm or your potatoes mushy. Cook until vegetables are fork tender. Season to taste, there are commercial stew seasoning packs available. Can add brown gravy mix or other thickeners for a richer and heavier sauce.

Soup with Stuff in It

When in doubt, simmer something. Even in warmer weather, people camping out can get cold, especially at night. Hot soup is a good thing (which is why there are several soup recipes in this book). You can take almost any liquid base, including water, and throw handy ingredients into to cook. The Vegan Vegetable Soup recipe is an organized and planned example of this, but the possibilities are almost endless. (For me, they end somewhere before you simmer poached eggs in hot cocoa.) So, start with water, tomato juice, vegetable broth, chicken broth, beef broth, or a thinned down condensed soup of any kind. Add ingredients you think might taste good that you have sitting around not defending themselves. Keep the classics in mind. If you have beef broth, add onions for French Onion Soup. (In ramekins, with croutons, and cheese broiled on top, this soup makes it a great day to be alive.) I like to use a condensed vegetable soup, add water or vegetable broth, whole kernel corn, and fresh onion, spiced heavily with red pepper flakes. Serve with broiled or toasted cheese bread. Take chicken broth, leftover chicken, carrots, and onions. Add salt, pepper, and maybe some chicken base. Throw wide egg noodles in 10 minutes before serving for a pretty classic version of Chicken Noodle Soup.

Minestrone

Pronounced with a long e on the end. A classic Italian soup. In Northern Italy (and in a lot of the versions sold in cans or restaurants), this is a thin soup with pieces of seasonal vegetables, maybe a few beans, and pasta (normally shells or macaroni), served in a vegetable or beef broth. In Southern Italy, and in the dry prepackaged mixes available here in the US, it is a thick bean stew, with tomato, ground meat (usually beef), and the pasta is broken spaghetti noodles. This is the version I grew up on, and the one I prefer. Take the dry minestrone mix (or any other dry multi bean soup mix, commonly sold as 13 bean soup, 15 bean soup, or 16 bean soup), rinse, and soak per instructions. Cook beans per instructions. 30 minutes before serving add drained, browned ground beef. Also add either crushed tomatoes or tomato juice per texture preference (I prefer the tomato juice). Season with Italian seasoning (basil, oregano, marjoram, thyme), garlic, and black pepper. 10 minutes before serving, add spaghetti noodles broken in quarter lengths. Garnish with grated Parmesan cheese and crackers. For me, the garnishes really make this dish, and I don't like it nearly as well without them. This is another hearty dish, appropriate for cold weather. One bag of beans and one pound of ground meat makes 8 to 10 bowls.

Vegan Vegetable Soup in 30 Minutes

Start with cans of mixed vegetables, on sale in any major grocery store. Pour in tomato juice, mixed vegetable juice, or vegetable broth. Use twice the liquid as the vegetable amount, at least. Per 2 servings, add one tablespoon of TVP, for protein, texture and bulk. Spice to taste (it probably has enough salt from the premade ingredients). I like to use basil, oregano, and black pepper, with a dash of hot sauce. If making small amounts (6 servings or less), this is ready in less than 15 minutes. Your carnivores probably won't hate this, even if they pretend to because it is Vegan. For non Vegans, goes well with loaves of French or Italian bread cut in half, topped with cheese, and broiled in the oven or toaster oven.

Best Beltane Recipe and Joke, Ever

Prepare miso soup mix per instructions. If you aren't familiar with it, miso is a Japanese soup with an earthy, salty flavor. Allow soup to cool, stir in honey, orange juice, pineapple juice, and teriyaki or soy sauce. Use this as a marinade for a pork roast, shoulder, or for extra fat and flavor, pork belly (where bacon comes from). Marinate for 24 hours in the fridge. While cooking, baste with leftover marinade. Large roast will take 2 hours or so at 375, covered. Can uncover last 15 minutes, the use of a meat thermometer is recommended to get pork to safe temperature. And this is the recipe for "Miso Honey for Pork." It is very good, so is the joke, and all versions of the dish are very sensual, rich eating experiences.

Split Pea Soup

Take one bag of dried green split peas. Rinse thoroughly and cook per instructions on the bag, stirring occasionally to prevent sticking. Cook until peas are soft and semi mushy. Take one leftover ham bone from a bone in holiday ham and put in 1 hour into cooking time (about halfway). If you don't have a left over ham bone, pre packaged ham cooking scraps work just fine. If you like carrots in split pea soup, add one carrot chopped into small pieces at the same time. I was taught a variation I like, which is to not use carrot, and wait until about 15 minutes before serving, then add one half of a large cooked sweet potato, peeled and chopped. Add lemon pepper, black pepper, and/or ham seasoning to taste. Can of course be made vegetarian by excluding the ham, but will require a lot more seasoning. One standard (1 lb) bag of peas makes 6 to 8 servings. If making in large batches of 20 servings or more, be extra careful avoid burning and sticking. This is a hearty, filling soup, appropriate for autumn or winter that people seem to really like or really dislike. It is very inexpensive, and reheats well. Most commercial (canned) versions of this soup are really bad, so encourage people to try it if they've never had the real homemade version.

Quick Pickled Vegetables with Rice

And while we're talking about Japanese food and rice, here's another idea. Take one part vinegar (either rice wine vinegar or white vinegar) to one part white sugar, stir until sugar is dissolved. In microwave safe bowl pour liquid over raw chopped or sliced vegetable pieces to cover. Can be used on peeled pieces of broccoli stem, cabbage, the whites of spring onions, cloves of garlic, or any other hard raw vegetable you like pickled. Microwave for 1 minute, then allow to cool to room temperature. Repeat until vegetables are crunchy, but softened to pickle consistency. It's best to prepare different vegetables separately because of varying firmness, but they can then be stored and/or served together. This will last in the fridge about 3 weeks. In Japan cold pickled vegetables are served over leftover room temperature rice as a breakfast meal. This may be a bit much for American stomachs at 8 AM, but a lot of people like this as a light summer lunch, or just a serving of the pickles as a snack.

Bean Salad with Pasta

This is a great, quick, and cheap vegetarian option, and is a perfect way to use up cold leftover noodles (you did dress them in EVO to prevent clumping, right?) or extra cans of beans you didn't need for chili. Also a good way to use those "unusual" canned beans that someone donated for chili but didn't really have the concept grasped fully. (I'm as big a fan of garbanzos/chickpeas as you are likely to find, but in chili? Really?) A variety of three different kinds of beans seems to be the standard. Serve cool, best with an oil/vinegar seasoned dressing (classic Italian works just fine). I've received good reviews on a version of this made with garbanzos, kidney beans, and crisp, just blanched green bean snaps, but it works just fine with a great variety of beans. If this recipe is being used as a side dish, assume the number of portions is half that of the dry noodle instructions on serving size for spaghetti or macaroni. For a vegetarian using it as a main dish, the portion is equal to what is listed on the box.

Chili Bake

In baking pan or casserole dish, layer chili, cheese (cheddar is good, as is casa fresca, or the "Mexican blend" sold in stores), and corn bread batter. For quickest time, used canned chili and be careful the cornbread layer is not too thick. Can be served with hot sauce on the side, sour cream and/or jalapenos. Instead of corn bread, can top the dish with corn chips (be careful not to burn them). This dish is also made with the cornbread on the bottom, and sometimes a layer of Mexican style rice is added (which I personally do not like, but I know is popular). 9" baking pan filled 3/4 to top will make 8 to 10 servings.

Quick Chili

Use canned beans such as prepared chili beans (usually cooked white beans in a chili sauce), red beans, black beans and/or kidney beans. Pinto beans can easily mush down and break apart (as in refried beans) so be careful if you choose to use them. Black beans do not give an appealing color to pale foods (black beans and rice taste delicious but are Nasty Looking), remember this when using them in chili. Use crushed tomatoes or sauce per texture preference, chopped onions, and ground meat (beef, pork sausage, turkey, venison). Most commonly used spices are chili powder, cumin, red pepper, black pepper, salt, and hot sauce or hot peppers to taste. Less common ingredients include molasses, tomatillos, beer, coffee, bell pepper, lentils or other exotic beans, ginger, and cinnamon. Dry packs and bottles of prepared chili seasoning are available. If you are using more than half the weight of the beans in meat, you are using too much meat for groups of 20 or more to be fed on a budget. Tell the people from Texas who say "If it has beans in it, it isn't chili" to keep their opinions under their big, stupid hats or match your food budget dollar for dollar. Assume a minimum of 8 oz per person.

Quick Chili Mac

Cook "spaghetti" noodles (see rant in the next recipe). Pour heated canned chili (can use beans only chili for vegetarians) on top of noodles as sauce. You can add extra red pepper, chili powder, or hot sauce to increase the heat if you like. Grate cheddar cheese on top. Serve with garlic bread.

Broasted (Twice Cooked) Potatoes

Here is another way to use the inevitable potato donations. Boil whole small to medium potatoes, in the skin, after checking for blemishes and removing "eyes." When potatoes are almost soft enough to serve, take off of heat. Blanch in cold water for quicker handling, or wait until cool enough to touch. Cut potatoes in half lengthwise into two "boats" that can lie flat with peel side down. If a boat is too unstable, cheat by slicing off enough of the bottom to ensure a flat seating. Brush tops with butter and/or gated cheese and broil in oven until golden brown. Easy to make, and with just a different enough texture from other preparations people really seem to like them. Normally, two halves are one side serving portion.

Fried Potatoes

This is an "any meal" recipe, people will eat it morning, noon, and night. Peel potatoes. And cut into thin slices, quarter slices for easy handling. Do the same thing with one onion per 5 or 6 potatoes. Using a fat in the pan (I like butter), stir potatoes and onions into skillet and brown potatoes at medium heat. Onions should be glassy and slightly browned. Use ham if desired (with me, it is desired a lot), country ham cooking pieces work well with this. Add a small amount of water, cover, and cook on low until potatoes and onions are soft, stirring at short intervals to keep food from sticking to skillet. This dish is easily made into a Vegan version by leaving out the ham and using a vegetable oil such as corn oil or olive oil. Salt and pepper to taste, allow one potato per person. Goes great at breakfast as side dish with fried or scrambled eggs, and makes a great side for pinto beans and cornbread in the afternoon and evening.

Quick Hash Browns

Grate potatoes in the coarse setting of your food grater. I prefer them peeled, but some people like "dirty" hash browns. Either chop onion, or grate it in the same setting as the potatoes for textural consistency. Use one onion per 5 potatoes. Add butter or oil to skillet or grill, fry on medium to high. For crispier, more browned hash, be sure all potatoes are touching the cooking surface at all times. When potatoes are browned on the outside they should be cooked tender on the inside. Salt and pepper to taste. Can be served with ketchup as a condiment. Traditionally, cheese, ham, or even chili can be added.

Spaghetti

To be technical, "spaghetti" is a noodle of a particular size and shape. In practice, Americans will use the name for any dish that has long thin noodles in a red sauce. Don't think Ramen noodles in ketchup doesn't count, I've seen it. A typical recipe is as follows: Brown ground meat, drain off excess fat. Stir in chopped onion and garlic to "sweat" until the onions are glassy in appearance. Add tomatoes or tomato sauce, per personal preference. After mixing ingredients add herbs and spices. This is normally basil, oregano, thyme, fennel seeds (I don't like them), black or white pepper, red pepper flakes, and sometimes marjoram. Many people add wine or balsamic vinegar. I was taught to add a little mustard (hot dog yellow or the fancy stuff) to a tomato sauce, and I like the results. I've had a very good sauce that had a little cinnamon in it. Many people add a sweetener, such as sugar, brown sugar, or honey. (I use molasses). Red wine or balsamic vinegar is also used to add flavor and cut the acidity of the tomatoes. Spaghetti seasoning is available as a dry blend in packs or bottles; prepared spaghetti sauce is available in cans or jars. Simmer sauce on low as long as you can. (Spaghetti sauce is almost invariably better the 2nd or 3rd day after serving it first). Cook noodles per package instructions (if you are feeding 20 or more people and making your own fresh noodles from scratch, you ate paint chips as a baby), "al dente" is usually the lowest listed time or even a minute or so less. For a gluten free version, serve sauce over prepared spaghetti squash or tofu noodles. Now, I absolutely love mushrooms in spaghetti sauce, but mushroom allergies are very common. Check in your group before using them, or at least be sure everyone knows they are in the sauce and be prepared to listen to the bitching. A quote from the Great and Powerful Lady Kelshei of the WynDragon Tradition of Wicca: "Are you allergic to them?" "No." "Then pick the f*ckers out."

Lasagna

In my experience, for best results, the noodles you choose and how you prepare them are vitally important. No bake lasagna noodles never give as a good a result. But the other horn of this dilemma is, if you follow the directions on the standard lasagna noodle box (cook for 11-14 minutes in boiling water), you end up with mushy noodles, and that isn't even looking forward to the leftovers. For best results, cook the lasagna noodles about one half of the suggested time (6 minutes or so). This will give you a fairly pliable noodle that will complete cooking while baking (this is a place where a thinner sauce can help. Use a basic red meat sauce, or marinara sauce, much as you would for spaghetti. In a pan at least 4 inches deep, layer sauce, lasagna noodles, and cheese. Putting a thin layer of sauce on the bottom as the first layer helps prevent the noodles from scorching, as does pouring a little sauce down the edges as layers are completed. I like to use a slightly thinner sauce for this than I do for spaghetti, partly for reasons mentioned above, and like a lot of people, I really like mushrooms in spaghetti but think they are weird in lasagna. It's a textural thing; if you don't get it, I can't explain it. So, from the bottom up, sauce, noodles, sauce, cheese, noodles, sauce, cheese, noodles, sauce, cheese on top. You can stack a lasagna as high as your pan will allow if you like it that way (many people do). Traditionally, the bottom cheese layer is a soft cheese layer, using a cheese such as ricotta, cottage, cheese, or a mixture of these two. Personally I like to use feta cheese for this, but it is a very strong cheese and a bit much for some tastes. At least one middle layer of cheese should be a hard but well melting cheese, such as mozzarella, provolone, or asiago. I have had a lasagna where cheddar cheese was used for this, it was old gym socks nasty. Blends, such as commercially available Italian blends or pizza blends work pretty well for this layer if you're getting a blend of real cheeses and not "processed cheese food product" (it says it on the package, swear to Lord and Lady). On the top, after you have put down the last sauce and hard cheese, cover with a hard browning cheese such as Parmesan, Romano, Cesare, or a blend. (Parmesan/Romano blends are available in canisters anywhere you buy Parmesan that way.) Cover with foil for half the cooking time or a bit more, then uncover so the top will brown a little, the edges will crisp, and the cheese will be bubbly. In my oven, usually about 45 minutes on 375 with the number of layers listed above. Lasagna is one of the things you should definitely cut into suggested portions, and serving it yourself is highly recommended. Good lasagna is so dense that people will take too large a portion and end up wasting food. As I've said, I'm perfectly happy to keep feeding people 2nds and 3rds as long as the dish holds out, but I don't want to do that until everyone else has had an opportunity to get a serving, and wanton waste p*sses me off. If you really want to push a lasagna over the top and give it a wow factor, prepare it exactly as per the recipe until you get to the top layer; before you put on the last layer of sauce and cheese put on a layer of half cooked meatballs on top. It's a lot of work to make both lasagna and meatballs for one dish, but it really is amazing. Not quite up for that, but want something a little different? A good variation is "Italian flag lasagna"; if you don't know the colors of the flag are red (sauce), white (noodles, cheese), and green (in this case a layer of fresh or precooked spinach). It sneaks in some nutrients they won't get otherwise, and adds some different texture and a depth of flavor. For "White and Green lasagna," a good vegetarian option, use a cream or cheese based sauce with spinach as opposed to a tomato sauce. A very popular vegetable lasagna that I have made (but did not invent the recipe), is made with a simple cream sauce that combines cream of celery soup (or another cream soup of your preference, like cream of mushroom), Italian seasonings, black pepper, garlic and milk. Can be combined cold and layered into the lasagna. Be very sparing with the sauce, especially on the bottom layers, or this will get very watery because of the fresh vegetables. Use cut fresh carrots (grated works just fine), zucchini and yellow squash chips and fresh raw spinach. Use these as separate layers except for combining the 2 kinds of squash. Don't have any lasagna noodles? Takes slices of eggplant, de seed them if the eggplant is large or older. Press liquid from eggplant, gently. After dipping in a milk or egg wash, coat thinly in flour, then fry crisp or until coating is golden brown in color. Drain on paper towels. Use the marinara sauce recipe and layer as you would a lasagna, substituting the eggplant slices for the lasagna noodles. This is called "Eggplant Parmesan" or "How to Get a Vegetarian Who Thinks You are Ugly to Sleep with You Anyway." This recipe will also work well with zucchini cut into chips. For someone with a wheat or gluten sensitivity, you can either brown the eggplant without a coating or use cornstarch in place of the flour.

Beef Stroganoff

Brown chopped roast or stew meat in hot pan with a small amount of Worcestershire sauce. When brown, add more Worcestershire until meat is mostly covered, simmer at medium to low heat for 45 minutes. Add mushrooms (if using fresh mushrooms, allow for longer cooking time before adding other ingredients). Add canned mushroom soup, and sour cream. When stirred together, add brown or mushroom gravy mix. Adding the soup, sour cream, gravy mix, and more Worcestershire sauce in layers helps produce a smoother sauce. When ready, this sauce is (not should be) thick enough to stand your stirring spoon vertically in the middle of the pot where it will stand upright for at least 30 seconds. This is a very rich and tangy sauce. Two tablespoons will flavor a serving of noodles or rice. I suggest serving it with extra wide egg noodles and a good, crusty bread for mopping up extra sauce. Like spaghetti sauce, stroganoff gets better after 2 or 3 days as the flavors continue to blend and build.

You can make a very good meatless version by using mushrooms only, cut into bigger pieces if desired. (Portobellos or shiitakes are good for this.) Remember to use a version of Worcestershire sauce that does not contain anchovies, and a brown gravy mix with no beef products.

Tuna and Noodles in Mushroom Sauce

Open and drain one can of tuna. Open one can of condensed cream of mushroom soup. Can use one small can of mushrooms, pieces and stems (optional). Stir together and heat in skillet. Can stir in mushroom gravy mix for thicker sauce. Serve over wide or extra wide egg noodles. Suggested serving size 3 oz (½ small can tuna) and 1 suggested serving of noodles per box. You can make one variation of this by using tuna and condensed cheese soup, but this is more expensive. Canned chicken, sometimes on sale at reasonable prices, cream of chicken soup, and chicken gravy mix can be used if you just don't like tuna. Again, it probably won't be quite as inexpensive as the first version, but it makes a nice change. Any of these can be served over rice instead of noodles. For further variation, add a small package of frozen peas to the tuna, soup and rice mixture, mixing thoroughly.

Meatballs

2 lbs ground meat (my preference is 1 lb Ground beef, ½ lb pork sausage, hot or mild your choice, and ½ lb ground turkey) to 1 lb cottage cheese large or small curd, whatever is cheaper, if same price get large curd for better aeration, 1 large (12 oz) box, crushed, of Cheese Nips or knock off (buy the cheapest knock off you can find, on purpose, they mix better), 2 large eggs, 1 large onion, chopped (optional), minced or chopped garlic, basil, oregano, can use Italian seasoning mix instead of herbal ingredients, black pepper. Combine all items in bowl. Do not over mix or you will make the meatballs tougher. Form into balls. For classic Sicilian style service, each meatball should be 2½ to 3 inches across, with one meatball cracked in half over pasta and then topped with sauce and cheese. Cover meatballs lightly in tomato sauce and bake until browned at edges and thoroughly cooked (approximately 35 minutes at 375, cover with foil for first 20 minutes). Recipe makes 16 -20 meatballs, or exact same recipe makes 2 bread loaf pans of meatloaf (increase cook time to 45 minutes, cover for first 30). In either case, a meatball or meat loaf recipe is designed to reduce portion costs with the use of filler. If you are using more than a 1 to 1 ration of meat to filler then you are defeating the purpose of the dish. The correct way to eat meatloaf is in cold slices on white bread with ketchup, all other answers are wrong, but partial credit can be given if served hot with brown gravy and mashed potatoes.

Meatloaf Topping

3 parts ketchup, 1 part Worcestershire sauce, 1 part molasses Mix thoroughly, pour on meatloaf, bake per instructions already given.

Quick and Dirty Meatloaf Gravy

Use packaged brown gravy mix, add pan drippings, can add 1 teaspoon ketchup and 1 teaspoon Worcestershire sauce per pack for "kick" otherwise prepare per instructions.

Sloppy Joes

Brown ground meat. Add tomato sauce, Worcestershire sauce, ketchup, chopped onions, black pepper, red pepper (optional), chopped green pepper (optional), brown sugar (optional), and garlic. You can choose to add the onions and green pepper first for longer cooking if preferred. Reduce until thick. Serve on hamburger buns. This works well with a beef/pork sausage blend, ground turkey, or a beef/TVP blend. This is great for summer events, and kids love it.

Barbecued Anything

OK, by the standards of snobs everywhere, including me, you are probably not going to make "real" barbecue at a gathering. Yes, you can rig a smoker if you are sufficiently handy (I am not). But, real barbecue takes forever, is expensive, and requires frequent hands on work (applying the "mop," etc.). If the last two sentences were complete gibberish to you, you don't need to be trying to do this the first time for this many people anyway. What you can do is take almost any flavorful piece of meat that you can get at a great price, put it in roasting pans, cover it in a sauce and cook it low and slow (low temperature for multiple hours). Baste frequently, serve with extra sauce. This works great for ribs or chops from beef, pork, or venison. It also works very well at a lower cost to use chicken thighs or turkey drumsticks. And, as is mentioned elsewhere in this book, this is a traditional method throughout Appalachia and the Southeastern US for preparing small game such as rabbit or squirrel.

"Repaired" Barbecue Sauce

This is quick, easy, and tastes good. Buy the cheapest BBQ sauce in the store. Combine 2 parts sauce with one part honey and one part Worcestershire sauce. You can add a little hot sauce, garlic and black pepper for a greater sense of accomplishment.

"Holy Cr*p, I Don't Have Any Barbecue Sauce" Barbecue Sauce

Using one of the numbers or letters style of steak sauce as a base, add ketchup or tomato sauce. Add small amounts of mustard, vinegar, Worcestershire sauce, and any sweeter, especially honey. In a pinch, canned soft drinks work just fine for the sweetener. Stir into pot, simmer until thick. Use hot.

Leftover Pizza

You made spaghetti, lasagna, and/or meatballs. Now you have leftover ingredients, like "red gravy" (classic Neapolitan style meat sauce for spaghetti), marinara sauce, extra cheese, mushrooms, meatballs, or cut vegetables. Using either freschetta, focaccia, premade pizza crusts, split loaves of French or Italian style bread, or even English muffins, layer on sauce, cheese, and other ingredients. If you have precooked ingredients (like meatballs), cook the pizza until crust is no longer raw and cheese is starting to melt, then add the ingredients that require less cooking time. For best use of meatballs, cut in half and place flat down so they don't roll. This is a great last minute panic attack dish when 10 extra people show up at the Gathering after dinner has been served. For much the same reason, even when the main dish for feast is lasagna, I always keep some spaghetti noodles on hand so that I can use the leftover sauce and feed someone in a hurry. This plan allows me to quickly serve someone who is lactose intolerant as well, since there are no dairy products in either the sauce or noodles.

"Filled" Corn Bread

To your normal corn bread batter or mix, add cheese (cheddar is best, Velveeta is traditional for Southern White Trash), whole kernel corn, and onions if desired (I don't like the onions in it, other people do). Bake per normal instructions, but remember bigger, deeper pans may take longer. Makes 6 to 8 servings.

Chunky Corn Pudding

To your normal corn bread batter or mix for 1 large skillet or muffin tin, add two cans creamed corn, cheese is optional. Bake until top and bottom are firm and golden brown, inside will be soft and semi liquid. Butter, salt, and pepper can be added to taste before or after cooking. Makes 6 to 8 servings.

Breakfast Bake

Use biscuit mix as prepared to box instructions or thin canned biscuits. This also works very well with canned crescent rolls spread out as the bottom layer. Grease pan to prevent sticking. Line bottom of baking pan with biscuit mixture. In bowl combine 12 eggs, cheese, and sausage (pre browned some, to remove grease and insure thorough cooking). One cook I know adds a can of condensed onion soup for extra flavor. You could add bacon and ham to live a little, if not necessarily for very long. Cook until browned on bottom and top, and solid all the way throughout the dish (350 for 35 minutes in my oven). Weirdly delicious with pancake syrup on it. Don't like biscuits or rolls even when disguised? Throw the mixture into a pastry shell, it makes a great quiche. A variation, not using biscuits or pastry, is to combine pieces of potato, onion, sausage and cheese into an egg mixture and bake. This can also be fried on the stove top, with or without the eggs, as a hash.

Eggy in a Basket

English favorite. Cut out the center of a piece of bread (a biscuit cutter works nicely, but so does any empty can of the right size. Put into a hot, buttered skillet. Pour 1 egg into the hole in the bread. You can put the skillet or a cookie sheet with several pieces into the oven to broil the top. For carnivores of a certain style, try "Eggy in a Piggy" and do the same thing but instead of bread, use a piece of bologna or (if you have money to burn) thick cut ham.

Banana Pancakes

Take your normal pancake recipe or mix. Reduce liquid amount slightly from recipe (bananas add moisture), and add mashed bananas, 1 banana per 2 servings. Makes moist, filling pancakes best served with banana syrup, and/or with freshly cut banana slices placed on top of the pancake stack before syrup is added.

Emergency Pancake Syrup

Take any sweetener (honey, Karo syrup, brown sugar). If solid, add water and stir until dissolved in a simple solution. If liquid, thin slightly with water. In either case, simmer on low heat until thickened to desired consistency. Serve hot on pancakes, waffles, or French toast. (This mixture will thicken past being able to pour if you let it cool for very long.) Can add spices or flavorings as desired. Sweet spices such as cinnamon, ginger, and nutmeg are commonly used, and fruit such as blueberries are added, with the solids being strained out before serving. When I was growing up, sliced bananas were added at the last minute before serving over banana pancakes.

French Toast

Bread too stale to taste good on its own makes perfectly good French Toast. Coat bread generously in egg wash (raw scrambled egg) and fry or grill in butter until both sides are golden brown. Either top with powdered sugar or pancake syrup. Goes well with a side of bacon, sausage, ham, or "facon." This recipe uses up stale bread and stretches a small amount of eggs into more servings of food. Allow one to two pieces per serving, French Toast is surprisingly rich and filling.

Dump Style Fruit Cobbler

Take a large disposable pan, like a roasting pan or serving pan, and dump in whatever fruit and/or liquid sweet filling you have. Cover with prepared biscuit batter, right out of the box, put one whole stick of butter cut into pieces at intervals on top, cook according to biscuit mix package for time and temp. Check the pan frequently to make sure it gets done and not burnt. One pan makes about 30 servings (cut them or serve them yourself if you think you might run out). I've had this made with canned cherry pie filling, canned apple pie filling, and fresh peaches cooked down in brown sugar. They all tasted good to me, and were popular desserts even when there were other options. All of them are of course at their best when served piping hot and topped with vanilla ice cream.

MTAQ
(MoonTurtle Asked Questions)

MoonTurtle is an aspiring Kitchen Witch who asked these questions to better understand the process of Kitchen Witching and the role of the Kitchen Witch.

Should the whole kitchen be made into sacred space?

This depends on the individual Kitchen Witch, as so many of these judgements do; but if you are going to make the whole kitchen sacred space you either need to consider making the boundary semi-permeable (as is done for rituals at many public gatherings), or physically blocking off the space. Without either of these options in place you will most likely end up with broken sacred space quite often, as, at least in my experience, people wander in and out of kitchens whenever they d*mn well feel like it, even when expressly told not to. (See the $1/50 cents Rule.)

Can Kitchen Witch tools be stored alongside other kitchen tools?

You are confronted with a set of basic issues our community has argued since before I was born. To what extent can a sacred tool be used as a mundane tool for mundane acts? If the act is consecrated (as I believe feeding our loved ones is), is any task performed in this manner mundane? Our community continues to be divided on this. Originally, bolines were used for all mundane acts needing a knife or cutting tool that led up to actual magical acts the athame was reserved for. But, I personally know many witches who cut string with the athame if the string is part of ritual, or prepare or eat food with their athame. However you decide these issues for yourself, be sure that someone will violently disagree with you. My gut feeling, personally, is that if your feelings are separating tools between kitchen witch tools and ordinary tools, then yes, you should store them separately. If they are all sacred, or ultimately all mundane, then store them together. In my experience, most self identified kitchen witches have a few tools (a knife, a wooden spoon, Grandma's iron skillet, etc.) that only they get to touch and that are stored separately. Again, there is a completely mundane "chef" answer for this as well; you don't want anybody f*cking up your best tools. I've seen favorite knives of cooks ruined by people who should never have been allowed safety scissors, let alone a knife. I've seen wooden spoons and cutting boards ruined through exposure to the wrong things and improper care. (Translation: "What dumb*ss put my wooden tools in water to soak overnight?") And it is literally a crying shame when someone ruins a properly seasoned iron skillet because they don't know what they are doing.

Is there any danger if magical items are used by others for mundane meals?

Again, this boils down to whether you consider there to be a fundamental divide. If there is a difference between magical and mundane meals for you, you might want to keep those magical tools with every other magical tool you don't share with the uninitiated for fear they would take harm from them. I have several tools reserved this way; thus the note that said "Do not touch Owl's altar, it will bite." For a lot of Kitchen Witches, however, all meals are magical and all cooks magicians, or even gods and goddesses of creation, so for them it is a non issue.

Are there any tools that should never be used in Kitchen Witching?

Well, shoes come to mind, but not much else. In all seriousness, if there are tools, just like certain foods or parts of animals in many traditional cultures, that to you are "profane," don't use them if you can manage not to. Some Kitchen Witches refuse to use plastic. I don't like using disposable items, especially for just one use. Styrofoam (polystyrene foam if we want to avoid the brand name) does not biodegrade well or quickly. But, for me personally, feeding the people at an event good food in a timely manner is more important than agonizing over the paper plates. If I have a choice in advance, it's not the choice I make. But I saw a community Elder make a complete *ss of himself by haranguing a group of people at their very first Pagan event for their use of disposable plates and cups, to the point that many of them never attended an event again, at least that I know of. The short form is; if you can pick your tools, great, if you can't, then pick your battles.

What essential tools should a Kitchen Witch always have or start with?

Good knives in a variety of sizes, specialized by task if you can. You need a knife for carving meat, a knife for chopping meat, a knife for chopping vegetables, a boning knife, and either a peeling knife or a vegetable peeler. A good quality steel food (cheese) grater, and I always put the cheese in parentheses because grating vegetables like carrots or potatoes lets you add their nutrition and flavor to a dish while decreasing the cooking time. A well stocked basic spice rack (you can purchase them that way). A good basic recipe book or set of recipe cards. For a community Kitchen Witch, a soup pot large enough to make soup for 10 to 15 servings over the number you think is the largest you will ever cook for; it will eventually turn out to be too small. At least one good iron skillet. A timer. A meat thermometer. A real potato masher or "ricer" depending on the texture you prefer. At least one honest friend who can taste the food and tell you if it sucks before 300 other people do. Love. Now, after the essentials there are few great things you'd like to have. A microwave oven (for reheating and certain shortcuts for time). A toaster and/or toaster oven. A rice cooker, the coolest, easiest way to cook rice on the planet. A good food processor or blender (a bad one is worse than not having one). A good quality roasting pan and/or dutch oven. A good set of metal mixing bowls. A good set of measuring spoons and cups. A good wire cutter for cheese and bread. (If you get a combination grater with wire slicer, it is probable that neither will be of the best quality.) An all metal meat grinder like your great grandmother had. Patience.

Is any special cleansing required after the initial cleanse and consecration? Can items be cleaned in the dishwasher? Is cleaning based on the item and what it was used for? What tasks would require special cleaning?

Like any other magical tool, periodic cleansing with intent keeps the bad woojy woojy away. I personally recommend cleaning any dishwasher safe items in the dishwasher, at least some of the time, as the high heat gets rid of stuff sink water just doesn't. With any tool you can clean in water, robes, altar cloths, kitchen tools, added salt is a great thing on occasion. Running the cleaned, dried tools through incense smoke would then complete a four element cleansing. Cleaning the item per its function and needs has been treated somewhat already, as a good way to ruin tools is to clean them incorrectly. I've seen a great knife, carbon steel and wooden handle, ruined by prolonged soaking, so, yes, you really do want to base cleansing on the item. If you are not familiar with a kitchen tool or gadget, always learn about it before you use it or clean it. Many kitchen witches will specially cleanse tools used to handle or prepare meat in any way. Others reserve this for items traditionally considered unclean in many cultures, like shellfish, pork, or offal. On the purely mundane level, especially for Kitchen Witches who are not used to handling food in quantities this large, extra care needs to be taken cleaning all tools, surfaces, clothes, and skin that touch raw meat, poultry, fish, or eggs.

Does the energy of dish continue after preparation, or will there be some present until the dish is consumed?

Most Kitchen Witches I know have trouble disconnecting from the food they prepare. If you can think of the preparation of the food as a ritual and then firmly and resolutely release the energy before serving it, then you will be much less likely to feel offended or hurt by criticism of the food (especially if you know it is unwarranted, mean spirited, or uneducated). Otherwise, you are absolutely right, if you can't manage to let the energy go then you will stay connected to it for an extended period of time.

Is there any special cleansing we should put ourselves through?

Thorough daily bathing is a great place to start. It is scary how filthy some of the people who want to handle food for dozens or hundreds of others actually are. If you can't bathe thoroughly every day at a gathering or festival, cleaning your hands thoroughly up to the elbows is a must before and after handling food, and if you don't have a nail brush, a Brillo pad will do. For spiritual cleansing; calming breaths, grounding and centering, followed by sprinkling yourself with salt water and then smudging with incense or sage is a good basic cleansing ritual before anything, if you can manage it. Otherwise, settle for the calming breaths and grounding and centering.

Are there any herbs we should always have on hand?

Always is a strong word, but there are few that I really am unhappy when I don't have them ready to use. I try to always have oregano, basil, thyme, marjoram, sage, and tarragon on hand. While some of these may not technically be herbs, I also try to keep cinnamon, nutmeg, cloves, allspice, salt, pepper (white and black), red pepper flakes, chili powder, mustard seed, ginger, garlic, and cumin available. For magical purposes, cooking sage still works for cleansing and protection, as does salt. Tarragon invokes the power of the Dragon, as do most "hot" herbs and spices. I don't tend to cook a lot with parsley, so it's not on my list, but if you have fresh parsley on hand you can give it to your help to chew and it will energize them with vitamins, help stave off colds from working in close quarters (and get rid of their stinky breath which is why you really give it to them in the first place).

Are there any herbs we should never use?

Again, never is a strong word, but as a Kitchen Witch in a public space, I try to have only those herbs and spices in the kitchen that are safe to breathe, handle, and consume in culinary (large) quantities. Now, safe is relative, and as mountain folk by blood and raising, I find a cold glass of sassafras tea to be very refreshing on a hot day. But the reason it's so refreshing is that it is a rather strong blood thinner, so while one glass is good, eight glasses are quite bad for you. A friend of mine gave herself an all over hematoma blood bruise as a child by drinking an entire pitcher at one sitting. The lesson here is that even with herbs safe to consume in relatively large quantities you want to understand there are dangers in over consumption. (Eat 5 large raw carrots every day, and you will turn your skin and urine orange, and the whites of your eyes yellow, in about 2 weeks. And you won't feel well at all.)

I personally try to keep small dose medicinal herbs such as willow bark, feverfew, and boneset out of a public kitchen. I also keep incense components, bath ingredients, or herbal dyes completely separate from the cooking area. At home you can keep these in your kitchen if you wish, provided everyone who will come in contact with them knows how to handle them correctly and that they are not for consumption. It just seems to me to be a bad idea to confuse people in a public space or take a risk with their safety I don't have to take. For the same reason, I try not have any decorative (but poisonous) plants in a kitchen or food prep area, and to avoid prepping food in areas with overhanging plants I don't recognize as safe.

What are pros and cons of organic?

(I know one con is cost for organic in comparison to non. But on the flip side organic is supposed to be better for us and the earth.)

You are correct, organic produce, meat, and dairy, is more expensive than products using otherwise widely accepted modifications and techniques. My issue with a lot of "certified organic" products has always been "Who watches the watchmen?" or "Who do you trust?" Do you trust the producers and distributers to be telling the truth? Is the product really organic? Or, are you paying for something you are not getting? With some products, the oversight is very strict and has been in place a long time. USDA inspectors make d*mn sure Choice US Beef is not sold as Prime. With others, if you don't know the providers personally, I've always been a little more skeptical. Also, if you are purchasing "organic" or "all natural" labelled products that have a multiple number of ingredients, read the fine print and be sure these are true for all ingredients. Organic products put less artificial ingredients into the earth, but several natural methods of farming are harsh to the land and people. Manure is fine for plants and for a lot of animals, but quite bad for people unless denatured really well. Clear cuttings, wetland drainage, and clearance by fire are all techniques used where chemicals are not. Again, for me, I want products that are good for planet and good for the community I am feeding, but I'm not always sure the labels are the whole story. I tend on staples and large quantity goods to try to buy local, and in season, but especially as a Kitchen Witch feeding large numbers of people at a time it really does come down to what I can get at a cost the Gathering can support.

Conclusion

As I said in the introduction, this work is a story. I hope it has been a useful story for you to read, and it has certainly been useful for me to tell it. I know the story isn't over, I have more of this story to keep learning myself. My hope is that this book serves as the opening chapters in your story about yourself as a cook, as a caretaker, as a nurturer, and as a Kitchen Witch. I hope it has made you laugh, and I'm pretty sure it must have p*ssed you off a time or two. My biggest hope is that this book has made you think, about yourself, about your own calling to serve others, and about just what it takes to undertake the physical support of a spiritual group or community.

Glossary of Terms

Ancestors, The: Our friends and family who have passed on. Many cultures set aside a time for honoring the ancestors. Samhain is the Sabbat when Wiccans and Pagans believe that the veil between the world and the afterlife are thinnest and it is a good time to remember and thank the ancestors for all the lessons and memories they have left with us. Candy and alcohol are common offerings to the ancestors, as is food that is a family favorite or a known favorite of the deceased.

Athame: Traditionally, the double edged, black handled ceremonial knife of the Witch. Usually made of iron or steel. In practice, for a Kitchen Witch, any knife or cutting instrument being used to prepare food in a sacred manner.

Avatar: In many faiths, an incarnate being, usually a human being, who shows one aspect or face of Divinity to the world while still remaining flesh. Many Wiccans and Pagans believe that all human beings either are, or have to potential to be, avatars, thus the use of the phrases "Thou art God" and "Thou art Goddess." In Wicca, the ability to aspect with conviction is usually a requirement for becoming a Priest or Priestess.

Boline: Traditionally, the white handled "prep" knife of the Witch, used for gatherings herbs or non sacred cutting. In practice for the Kitchen Witch, mostly a non sequitur, as all cutting with the knife is holy and thus the job of the athame.

Book of Shadows (and of Light), The: The Traditional journal, spell book, and for this book especially, the recipe book of a Witch, Wiccan, or Kitchen Witch. If you don't write down the change you made to the recipe, you will forget why it was so good (or so bad). If you don't keep your recipes and experiences ordered somewhere in some way, in print, it is much harder to learn from them. This is the collective opinion of generations of Witches, and my opinion as well.

Cakes: The token of food (representing the God) blessed in ritual along with the Cup. Usually a grain product like bread, the cake can be anything ritually or seasonally appropriate, like cheese for Imbolc and meat for Samhain.

Calling, The: Used both in religious and secular situations. To hear the calling or have a calling is to have a vocation, religious or otherwise. The term is frequently used where the vocation is either in religious service or serves the community in a secular way. So, you will hear that someone was called to the priesthood, or had a calling to be a doctor.

Cleansing: Cleaning and preparation for holy work and/or attending rituals. The mundane part of this, very important for food preparation, is thoroughly and frequently bathing, followed by washing hands up to the elbows before and after all food handling. For all kitchen tools, wash thoroughly in very hot water with dish soap. The spiritual part of this can include sprinkling with salt water, running the smoke of incense or sage over the Kitchen Witch and the tools to be used, making the kitchen calm and orderly, and for the Kitchen Witch to attain a calm mindfulness from which all food preparation can be done with love.

Coven: The common name for a formal and hierarchical group of witches or Wiccans, traditionally made up of 13 people, led by a High Priestess, frequently with the aid of a High Priest. Now used to describe somewhat less formal groups as well.

Cup, The: The liquid (representing Goddess) blessed as part of ritual. Traditionally wine, it can be anything ritually or seasonally appropriate, like milk at Imbolc. In groups where alcohol is an issue either a non alcoholic Cup or two Cups may be offered.

Elders: This can be a confusing term as it has three basic meanings normally used in the Pagan and Wiccan community with people rarely stopping to explain which one they are using when referencing an individual. It is used to refer to an individual who has achieved a knowledge or initiatory leadership status within the community. It is used to refer to someone who has undergone a sacramental acknowledgement of late adulthood, which depending on gender is usually referred to as a Croning or a Saging, after which the individual is referred to as an Elder, Crone, or Sage. It is also used in its simplest form to refer to older members of the community who may have special physical needs due to age.

Feast, The: This term is sometimes used for the main, most important meal at an event or gathering, the rest being soups, sandwich fixings or snack trays. At other events, "feast" is a term used interchangeably with "dinner" or "supper," and is the most ritually important meal of the day, but not of the event. This term was probably stolen fair and square from the Society for Creative Anachronism, the SCA for short.

Feast Gear: The fancy Pagan or Wiccan term for plates, bowls, cups, and utensils, collectively; in short, everything an individual needs to eat a meal. This term was probably stolen fair and square from the SCA.

Feng Shui: The Chinese geomantic art that combines home or business placement, room placement within a structure, general architectural design and interior decoration to produce a stress free and positive environment.

Fey, The: The faerie folk, fairies. The beings of magic on the other side of the veil of possibility and wonder. This veil is thinnest at Beltane (May Day). Milk, cream, and honey (especially on the comb) are common food offerings left for the Fey. Some households reserve a special bowl for this, just like they do for the Lady's Plate.

Gathering: A large retreat where Pagans and/or Wiccans from different groups gather to together to celebrate a holiday or hold a ritual, usually held in honor of one the eight Sabbats. Cooking for this many people is what requires a Kitchen Witch as a specialized path or calling. Also called gathers or festivals. In practice, gatherings are usually weekend events, starting on Friday and ending on Sunday. Very large events can last most of a week and start on Wednesday or Thursday.

Gathering, 2nd definition: The process of gleaning wild fruits, roots, herbs, etc. For very Traditional peoples who do not practice agriculture, the only source of non animal based foods.

Gathering Coordinator: A Kitchen Witch is (normally) a Gathering department head, in charge of this specific area of the Gathering's functions. The Gathering Coordinator is in overall charge of the event, coordinating food, site issues, cleanup, registration, and all other needs. Other standard departments besides the kitchen include registration, security, vending, site, and medical.

Grounding and Centering: Grounding is when you visualize reaching down into the earth, sending roots, like a tree seeking the calming energy of the world. Centering, done with the visual image of stretching leaves like a tree, or wings like a bird, is reaching up into the sky and cosmos for the clear clean energy of the universe. Usually done together, grounding and centering can be calming, meditative, relaxing, and energizing all at the same time. As a technique it takes two minutes to learn and a lifetime to master. A great calming technique for those who spend time in chaotic environments (like kitchens).

Lady, The: The Goddess, the female face of Divinity as worshipped by many Pagans and Wiccans when a more specific form is not used.

Lady's Plate, The: The offering to the Lady and the Lord made with samples of the food provided for the feast. Sometimes also used to refer to the specially reserved (and sometimes consecrated) plate on which the offering is made.

Lord, The: The God, the male face of Divinity as worshipped by many Pagans and Wiccans when a more specific form is not used.

Magic: The metaphysical art of changing reality by the application of belief and will.

Medical: The nice people who take care of your boo boos. If you make sure the Kitchen Witch knows your dietary restrictions, you actually abide by your dietary restrictions, and if necessary provide some or all of your own food to meet these restrictions, you are less likely to need the services of the nice people in Medical.

Pagan: In modern usage, describes a believer in one of several Nature based faiths where reverence of the earth and a belief in magic as a force for positive change are cornerstone values.

Registration Coordinator: The individual primarily responsible for making sure everyone is signed in and has paid to attend the event. Registration also has emergency contact information and medical information. A lot of times, the Kitchen Witch will receive notification of food reactions, sensitivities, or allergies from Registration, and not directly from the individual.

Sabbat: One of the 8 major holidays celebrated annually by Wiccans and many other Pagans. These occur at the equinoxes, the solstices, and at the midpoints between, approximately one Sabbat every 6 weeks. The Sabbats are Yule (Winter Solstice), Imbolc (Groundhog Day), Ostarra (Spring Equinox), Beltane (May Day), Litha (Summer Solstice), Lughnassa, Mabon (Autumnal Equinox), and Samhain (Halloween).

Wiccan: Follower/believer of the religion of Wicca, the best known of the modern Pagan faiths. In older usage, only used to describe someone who has been initiated to at least the first of the three degrees.

References/Suggested Reading

Some these books are listed here because of their Pagan and Wiccan perspectives on food and how to treat it in a sacred manner, including the ritual use of herbs. There are books listed here with food blessings and prayers. I've also listed books that explore vegetarian options and money saving techniques, both invaluable for the Kitchen Witch. Others are listed for cooking techniques and basics, or just because some of the recipes are just so d*mn good.

Recipes from a Vegetarian Goddess by Kari Allrich

Meal by Meal by Donald Altman

Vaughan's Vegetable Cook Book (4th Edition) How to Cook and Use Rarer Vegetables and Herbs by Anonymous

Gentle Eating by Stephen Arterburn, M. Ed., Mary Ehemann, and Vivian Lamphear

*Get in the Kitchen, B*tches* by Jason Bailin

The Master Book of Herbalism by Paul Beyerl

Witchcraft on a Shoestring, Ch. 7, "Feeding the Masses" by Deborah Blake

The Khaki Kook Book a Collection of a Hundred Cheap and Practical Recipes Mostly from Hindustan by Mary Kennedy Core

Magical Herbalism by Scott Cunningham

The Magic in Food: Legends, Lore and Spells by Scott Cunningham

Kitchen Witchery by Marilyn F. Daniel

Fit for Life by Harvey and Marilyn Diamond

A Cordiall Water: A Garden of Odd and Old Receipts to Assuage the Ills of Man and Beast by M. F. K. Fisher

How to Cook Wolf by M. F. K. Fisher

Psychic Self Defense by Dion Fortune

Pagan Feasts: Seasonal Foods for the Eight Festivals by Anna Franklin and Sue Phillips

Good to Eat: Riddles of Food and Culture by Marvin Harris

The Healing Foods by Patricia Hausman and Judith Benn Hurley

The Rodale Herb Book ed William H. Hylton

The Mafia Cookbook by Joseph Iannuzzi

World of the East Vegetarian Cooking by Madhur Jaffries

Simple Japanese Cooking comp The Japanese Cooking Companions

Raw Vegan Recipes 1 and 2 by Kevin Kerr

Kitchen Herbs and Spices by D. Lanska and B. Hlava

All New Sophie Leavitt's Penny Pincher's Cookbook by Sophie Leavitts

The Slim Gourmet by Martin Lederman

The Chinese Vegetarian Cookbook by Gary Lee

Chinese Vegetarian Cooking by Kenneth H. C. Lo

The Japan Diet by Naomi Moriyama and William Doyle

Bud, Blossom, and Leaf: The Magical Herb Gardener's Handbook by Dorothy Morrison

Words of Light and Midnight: Poems From a Pagan Priest by P. B. Owl

Cassell's Vegetarian Cookery a Manual of Cheap and Wholesome Diet by A. G. Payne

Food by Susan Powter

The Higher Taste: A Guide to Gourmet Vegetarian Cooking and a Karma Free Diet by A. C. Bhaktivedanta Swami Prabhupada et al.

Nanny Ogg's Cookbook by Terry Pratchett

The Pagan's Muse: Poems of Ritual and Inspiration ed Jean Raeburn

30 Minute Meals by Rachael Ray

30 Minute Meals 2 by Rachael Ray

A Garden Of Herbs by Eleanour Sinclair Rohde

Salt Free Cooking with Herbs and Spices by June Roth

The Book of Tofu by William Shurtleff and Akiko Aoyagi

Witches' Brew by Patricia Telesco

Witch in the Kitchen: Titania's Book of Magical Feasts by Titania

The Wicca Cookbook: Recipes, Ritual, and Lore by Jamie Wood and Tara Seefeldt

The Wiccan Herbal: Recipes, Magick, and Abundance by Jamie Wood

Cook This, Not That by David Zinczenko and Matt Goulding

About the Author

P. B. Owl holds a 3rd Degree through the WynDragon Tradition of Wicca, and also serves as an Elder in this Tradition and in the Moon's Inkwell, CeltiaDraconis and Ring of Bright Water Traditions of Wicca. Since 1995, his articles (as P. B. Owl) and poetry (some appearing under the byline Burrowing Owl) have appeared in "Paganet News", "13 Moons", "Waxing and Waning", "Fagan", "WynterGreen", "The Starlight Gathering", "GreenEggzine" and THE PAGAN'S MUSE (ed Jane Raeburn, Citadel Press).

He is a founding member of the WynDragon Family, an East TN based Wiccan seminary founded in 1999, where he serves as Man in Black.

He has served as a Kitchen Witch at events and gatherings throughout the SouthEast since 1998.

His first Pagan or Wiccan book, **Words of Light and Midnight: Poems from a Pagan Priest**, was released in September 2013 by BlackWyrm Publishing. This is his second Pagan or Wiccan book.

www.ingramcontent.com/pod-product-compliance
Lightning Source LLC
Chambersburg PA
CBHW061505040426
42450CB00008B/1494